The Honest to God Church

The Honest to God Church

A Pathway to God's Grace

Doug Bixby

THE
ALBAN
INSTITUTE
Herndon, Virginia
www.alban.org

The Alban Institute
2121 Cooperative Way, Suite 100
Herndon, VA 20171

Scripture quotations, unless otherwise noted, are from the New Revised Standard Version of the Bible, © 1989, Division of Christian Education of the National Council of Churches of Christ in the United States of America, and are used by permission.

Cover design by Wendy Ronga, Hampton Design Group.

Library of Congress Cataloging-in-Publication Data

Bixby, Douglas J., 1967-
  The honest to God church : a pathway to God's grace / Doug Bixby.
    p. cm.
  Includes bibliographical references (p.   ).
  ISBN 978-1-56699-344-9
  1. Church management. 2. Conflict management—Religious aspects—Christianity. 3. Christian life. I. Title.

BV652.9.B63 2007
253--dc22
                              2007013580

    11   10   09   08   07   UG   1   2   3   4   5

To my parents, Jim and Karen Bixby,
with gratitude for all their love and support.

Contents

Foreword

All over North America, churches and their leaders are coping with Christendom's ruin. Some churches have simply stepped out of the ruins and are doing something new and different. Others live and work amid the ruins, busily sifting out what is precious from what is expendable. Still others do not seem to notice the ruins that surround them at all. They pretend that things are pretty much the same as they always been, and that we can do church as we always have done it.

Christendom, and its American version, was like every other era of the church. It had both strengths and weaknesses. Sometimes the two were pretty much the same. In the heyday of Christendom and of the more mainline Protestant denominations, church was a place for society's leaders, doers, and givers. It was a place for folks who had it together. This was, in many ways, a strength. During Christendom great institutions were built, and not only churches. Universities, colleges, seminaries, service agencies, hospitals, YMCAs and YWCAs, mission programs, and more dot the landscape of Christendom and mark its achievements. But this very strength was also, and in another way, Christendom's weakness. If the church in the Christendom era welcomed and encouraged our noble selves, it did not always welcome or encourage our real selves.

When it came to grace, we talked a good line, but often it was good works and achievement that we believed in. We pointed to the numbers: numbers of members, numbers of dollars given to mission, numbers in the Sunday school and the youth ministry, and the statistical evidence of our good deeds for validation. But grace, however much we sang or preached of it, wasn't what we lived by or on. And so what happened is what always happens: God brought us to our knees to learn our need of God, our need of mercy, and our utter dependence on grace.

Doug Bixby invites us to bring our real selves to church and to God. He shows us ways to move through and beyond the ruins of Christendom and into a new time and a different church. He shows us what the church and the life of discipleship look like when we get honest with God and get real with one another.

In helping us to make such moves and take such steps, Doug does not draw on either New Age happy talk or megachurch technique. Doug does what those in the business of new life and renewal have always done: he goes back to the roots, to the source, and to the heart of the gospel. He goes back to grace, to God, and to what God has done in Jesus Christ. He goes back to the ways of God with us and among us. But by going back, he helps us to go forward in a time that is often challenging and at times discouraging. In doing so, Doug reminds us why we are here at all and of the peculiar and particular gift that God would give the world through the church.

The Honest to God Church: A Pathway to God's Grace is a splendid work of pastoral theology. It is pastoral because it is grounded in real life and in the lives of real people. It is written by someone who loves the church and believes in it. Moreover, Doug writes in a wonderfully accessible style. He is not trying to impress anyone with big words or fancy references. He is writing to be read and understood. He is writing to provoke prayer and evoke conversation. He is writing to be helpful to the church in a new time. And yet it is also true that *The Honest to God Church* is a work of theology. The heart of the gospel beats steadily in this book. Without ever getting lost in arcane theological thickets, Doug walks the solid ground of gospel truth.

I hope that many congregations will read this book either as a study/discussion book for the whole church or in small groups and adult classes. It is a book that promises to be helpful in three particular and crucial areas of church life today: hospitality, spirituality, and discipleship.

The hospitality of the church is not simply a matter of being nice or of being really friendly. Nor is hospitality accomplished by better signs, name tags, or a really great coffee hour. Hospitality is about grace. It is about welcoming others, whoever they are, wherever they are on life's journey, because that's the way God welcomed us. It is about loving others because God has loved us. In practicing such gracious hospitality and welcome, some tough questions will be encountered. Are there conditions? Prerequisites? Doug faces those tough questions honestly and graciously as he draws on examples from his pastoral experience.

Second, this is a book about Christian spirituality. Ironically, in the Christendom era, not many books were written about spirituality other than those by Roman Catholics. There wasn't much encouragement for tending one's soul or acknowledgment of the hand-to-hand combat being waged between the ego and the soul in many believers' hearts and in most of our churches. Doug gets into the real stuff of spirituality, including sin and shame, pride and pain, grace and healing. He probes the depths of grace to find new dimensions for our time and for our lives.

Third (I won't say "finally," because chances are good that you will find more in this rich book than these three important themes), this book is about discipleship. What does it mean to be a disciple, to grow as a disciple, and to live as a disciple of the gracious Lord Jesus? Doug provides pointers and prompts for the journey. He never reduces discipleship to a formula or a recipe, but he does challenge us to take the next step.

Action steps are provided throughout the book. For the most part, these are ordinary and unspectacular things, and readers

may react to them as the Syrian general Naaman reacted to the
instructions of the prophet Elisha (see 2 Kings 5). Naaman really
expected Elisha to do something way, way cool and imagined that
he himself would be sent on a quest of heroic dimension to have
his leprosy cured. Elisha sent word by messenger to Naaman,
"Go, wash in the Jordan seven times." To the great Naaman, this
"action step" seemed neither hard enough nor exotic enough.
He wanted something really challenging, something that would
allow him a sense of accomplishment. Naaman was not flattered
by Elisha's instructions. But that was the point: not flattery, but
humility.

Thank heavens, Naaman's servants managed to persuade the
great man to heed the prophet's instructions, to do the simple
(if not easy) thing of getting down into the Jordan's muddy water. So Doug Bixby's action steps and discipleship steps do not
entail long journeys to exotic places, great feats of theological
knowledge, or valiant acts of heroic service. They ask only that
we take the next step and see where it leads, see where Christ
leads.

In poet T. S. Eliot's famous lines, "We shall not cease from
exploration. And the end of all our exploring will be to arrive
where we started and know the place for the first time." I have a
feeling that something like this is what the readers of this book
will experience.

Anthony B. Robinson
Author of *What's Theology Got to Do With It?*
Convictions, Vitality and the Church

Preface

"**W**as Jesus a liberal or a conservative?" This is one of my favorite questions to ask when I speak at Christian conferences. The typical response is a short period of stunned silence. Then someone in the middle of the room usually shouts out, "Neither." Another person usually follows by shouting, "Both." The truth is that the modern categories of liberal and conservative do not work well when describing Jesus. Therefore, I contend that they should not be used to describe his disciples or churches. Categories such as these limit our spiritual growth and keep us from being the kind of disciples Jesus desires. Extreme conservative and liberal Christians often focus more on being conservative or liberal than they do on being followers of Jesus. The purpose of this book is to help churches and Christians develop an alternative approach to Christianity between the liberal and conservative extremes.

Many people in our society have grown tired of the extremes. Numerous individuals have shared with me their frustrations of feeling boxed in spiritually by the categories of liberal and conservative. They desire an approach to Christianity that is passionate about Jesus but unrestricted by these modern terms. Conservative and liberal labels make it easy for churches and denominations to define themselves without focusing on Jesus and his expectations of us. The extent to which these terms have divided the church in this age is disturbing. Through this book, I offer a clear, distinct alternative between these two extremes. The alternative is not wishy-washy or boring but, rather, a bold form of grace-based discipleship. I encourage readers to pursue a passionate new direction and approach to the Christian faith. Liberal and conservative constructs are mere crutches holding up the right and left sides of the church. We would be stronger if we could learn how to walk on our own two feet and follow Jesus without these crutches.

The strong division between liberals and conservatives in the church today demonstrates how dysfunctional the church has become. Between the two extremes of chaos and rigidity, there is a healthy middle ground. In offering an alternative to liberal and conservative extremes in the church, I am, in essence, advocating an older approach—the art of following Jesus. As Christians we should seek to value what Christ valued and to make a priority the things that mattered most to him. Honesty, humility, and grace are a few central themes that emerge from Jesus's approach to life as demonstrated in his earthly ministry. This book provides some key spiritual strategies we must incorporate into our lives and churches if we hope to develop an effective alternative approach to discipleship and being the church.

This book also takes a good hard look at how God's grace can help us to develop open and honest environments within our churches. I encourage people to become more honest with themselves, God, and others in life and at church. And I urge them to recognize the value of grace for their lives and ministries. God's grace heals, forgives, and strengthens us as we seek to follow Jesus humbly and honestly between the extremes. Sin, shame, and pain lie at the root of spiritual dysfunction in our lives and our churches. We often seek to hide these realities behind a facade of perfection, which historically the church has reinforced. We will examine how each one of these realities impacts our lives and congregations.

This book is presented in two parts. Part 1 is "Honest to God Churches." These chapters focus on how church leaders can develop a between-the-extremes approach to life within their congregations. Action steps are listed at the end of each of these chapters. Part 2 is "Honest to God Disciples." These chapters focus on developing an open and honest approach to Christian discipleship. Discipleship steps are listed at the end of each of these chapters to help readers with spiritual formation. And discussion questions for personal reflection or small group discussion can be found at the end of every chapter. This book may be used by small groups or leadership teams. My hope is that it will give readers a desire to pursue an alternative approach between the extremes where honesty, humility, healing, and faith can flourish. I hope it will be a pathway to grace.

Acknowledgments

I would like to thank and acknowledge those who have helped make this book possible. I cannot say enough about the support I have received from my wife, Carolyn. Her encouragement, editing, and honesty helped make this book what it is. She is also a great mother, and sharing my life experiences with her makes everything in my life more meaningful. I also want to thank my daughters for who they are and how much joy they bring into my life. They inspire my writing and me. They are wonderful daughters, and few things feed my soul like the time I spend with my family.

I also want to thank the people of Salem Covenant Church. I began writing this manuscript while on a three-month sabbatical granted me after serving ten years as their pastor. This sabbatical gave me the opportunity to pull together the ideas and insights I gained during these ten years and the three years I spent at North Park University. This book was waiting to be written. I wrote two hundred pages of manuscript in my first two weeks of sabbatical. I then began the hard work of editing, restructuring, and cleaning up what I had written. Clearly this sabbatical and my experiences at Salem Covenant Church helped to make this book a possibility.

I also want to say a special thanks to my editor, Kristy Pullen, and the Alban Institute for believing in this book and helping me to prepare it for publication. Their advice and encouragement have been much appreciated.

Finally, I want to thank all the people who have helped shape this book through the life experiences I have shared with them. I want to thank all my family and friends, especially those who have given me permission to share their stories in these pages. Many people have given shape to my life and, thus, have directly and indirectly contributed to this book. Having my work published is a humbling experience for me. It is an honor to share my thoughts and ideas about the church and Christian discipleship with you.

Introduction

*W*hile *driving with my family from our home in Connecticut* to the Outer Banks of North Carolina for a family reunion and beach vacation, I could not help but notice how bold the church signs were getting along the way. Every church wanted to make a statement. One church had their name and "fundamentalist, independent, and Bible believing" all on their sign. This church seemed to take themselves too seriously. Another church affiliated with a mainline denomination posted a sign saying, "Mindless Worship Is Meaningless Worship." This church seemed to be angry about something. Another church meeting in an old warehouse had a sign that said, "Come as You Are," plastered on the front of their building. This sign caught my attention. This church obviously understood that most people driving by their building on a Sunday morning were heading for the beach, not church. They understood that people were driving by in bathing suits, shorts, T-shirts, and sandals. A statement such as "Come as You Are" is quite inviting in this context. But were my assumptions correct? Did this church really want people to come as they were, or were they just willing to let people in beach clothes attend their services?

Too many churches want their people to pretend when they walk through the church doors. People often behave one

1

way in church and another way at home or work. Even worse, inauthentic Christians may try to bring a superficial form of Christianity into their neighborhoods, schools, communities, and workplaces. Jesus loved it when people came to him as they were. Think about the woman with the hemorrhage, the Samaritan woman at the well, and Zacchaeus, the chief tax collector. These stories and many others reveal that Jesus valued real encounters with real people facing real life struggles. Honest to God churches invite people to come as they are. They want their people to be honest with God, themselves, and one another.

At "Come as You Are" parties the host makes all the preparations ahead of time. The refreshments are prepared and set out. The entertainment is secured. The room is decorated. Everything is done ahead of time—except the sending of invitations. Guests are invited just as the party is about to begin. And they are asked to "come as they are" at the time of the phone call. People in sweatpants and T-shirts come as they are. Those who have been working outside and have on dirty clothes come as they are. Couples dressed to go out for a nice dinner come as they are. Whatever the circumstances of one's life at the time of the phone call determines how a person will look when he or she comes to the party. I think Jesus would like these parties. Jesus does not ask us to cover up anything in our lives. Covering up only serves to help us avoid intimacy with one another and with God.

If all churches allowed people to be more honest, we would not struggle with as many of the issues as we struggle with in our local churches today. If churches truly allowed people to be more honest with God, our churches would be more inviting to a far broader range of people. If church members gave themselves permission to be more honest, God would be able to work more freely in their lives. God does not want us to put up facades. He wants us to be honest with him and with one another.

Sin, shame, and pain are three of the primary reasons Christians hide behind facades within their spiritual lives. In the following pages, we will explore these and other reasons why Christians are afraid to be honest, and I will offer pathways for churches and individuals to begin living in more authentic Christian ways. God is good, and he wants what is best for our churches and for us. God wants us to become more honest with him and with each other. Transparency with God can help to rehabilitate us and revolutionize our world. Being honest with God is about being real and about the real things that will happen to us while we worship, minister, study, and pray with one another in this context.

Part One

~~~~~

Honest to God Churches

One

Grace and Graciousness

I have a friend who converted from the Jewish faith to the Christian faith. He shared, however, that he had also become disenchanted with Christianity as a result of a bad experience. He described how after becoming a devoted Christian he visited a Pentecostal church and enjoyed its worship style tremendously. He said that he actually spoke in tongues during his first visit to the church. Then he said the preacher got up to preach and spewed forth what he called "toxic judgmentalism" all over the congregation. This preacher was defining Christianity in terms of who was not allowed to participate. My friend described how he went from a spiritual high to a spiritual low in a matter of minutes. He shared that his perception of Christianity has never been the same since. He said the only truly positive Christian experience he has had since then was on a visit to a Catholic monastery where a monk said, "Everyone is welcome because Jesus excluded no one."

Grace

In the church we talk about having faith and being faithful, but rarely do we talk about experiencing grace and being gracious.

Churches are actually at times some of the most ungracious places on this planet, and Christians are at times some of the most ungracious people in our universe. If as Christians we boldly claim to be the recipients of God's grace and mercy, doesn't it make sense for us to respond by being equally gracious and merciful? If grace is the method God chose for ministering to us, shouldn't it be the method we use to minister to one another? If grace is good enough for God, should it not also be good enough for us? How is it that the church, which has been built on the foundation of God's mercy, has become so merciless?

I fear that the church has become the unforgiving servant from Jesus's parable. The unforgiving servant was a slave who could not settle his accounts and, therefore, had to be sold along with his family and all their possessions. The servant pleaded with his master to forgive his debt, and his master obliged. But when a fellow slave came to the forgiven servant owing a much smaller amount of money and asked that his debt be forgiven, the servant refused. Instead, he had him thrown in prison until the debt was repaid. After hearing what had transpired, the master summoned his servant and said, "You wicked slave! I forgave you all that debt because you pleaded with me. Should you not have had mercy on your fellow slave, as I had mercy on you?" (Matt. 18:32–33).

As Christians we claim to receive God's grace and mercy through Jesus Christ. The time has come for us to show grace and mercy to one another. But how do we change the way our churches function so that our congregations become more gracious? In response to this challenge, the church I pastor, Salem Covenant Church, in Washington, Connecticut, has sought to develop what I call an "I'm not okay, you're not okay" approach to Christian ministry. This approach embraces an ethic of love and takes the commandment to "love your neighbor as yourself" very seriously. It is an open approach that allows people to be honest about who they are and about their sinfulness and brokenness. It is the means by which congregations can effectively become honest to God churches. This approach is very different from the two other approaches that churches have traditionally taken.

Many churches have tried the "I'm okay, you're not okay" approach. Christians using this approach see themselves as okay, while everyone outside the church is not okay. Churches embracing this approach embrace an ethic of perfection rather than love. Often they are very judgmental and rigid. Very little room exists for grace after a person is converted. Legalism, rather than love, becomes the primary defining characteristic of these churches. It is not wrong to strive toward perfection. A problem exists, however, when people pretend to be perfect even though they are not. This is the approach that most fundamentalist churches and many evangelical churches take.

In response to this approach, many liberal mainline churches have inadvertently taken the "I'm okay, you're okay" approach. In these churches, Christians do not expect much from anyone, even themselves. They replace judgmentalism with an ethic of tolerance. But an ethic of tolerance is not the same as an ethic of love. Tolerating someone is not the same thing as loving them. Love is deeper and more significant. Tolerance demands only that we give people space. Love demands that we enter into their space. Besides, if on our own we are okay, why do we need to be part of a church? If we are already okay, then why do we need God and one another?

I recommend the "I'm not okay, you're not okay" approach. This approach embraces the teaching of Martin Luther that we all are saints and sinners simultaneously. Churches following this approach raise disciples who readily admit to the mess within their lives. They admit to their sin and brokenness and see God's grace as the only means for straightening out their lives. With this approach, we do not have to pretend that we are okay when we are not; we do not have to fool others into thinking that we are perfect. In these churches, we are asked to come as we are between the extremes.

So, on the one hand, an ethic of perfection leads to intolerance, which leaves little room for grace. On the other hand, an ethic of tolerance leaves too much room for ambivalence and, therefore, does not see any need for grace. Tolerance is better than judgment, but love is deeper and more able to transform our lives than either tolerance or judgment. Jesus's ethic of love leaves room not only for grace, but also for graciousness. Grace is the gift of God's forgiveness, acceptance, healing, and transformational power. Graciousness is the gift of respect, forgiveness, and acceptance that we offer each other. We offer graciousness when we seek to understand others before judging them. Therefore, beneath the ethic of tolerance and perfection lies the ethic of love, guided by Christlike compassion, and dominated by Christlike action. Jesus said, "By this everyone will know that you are my disciples, if you have love for one another" (John 13:35).

Embracing the "I'm not okay, you're not okay" approach takes honesty, courage, and vulnerability. It enables us to acknowledge that it is not us, but God, who is righteous. God is perfect, and through the process of redemption, he is perfecting us by his perfect love. This approach invites us into an open and honest redeeming relationship with Christ in which we are allowed to be ourselves. There is no "bait and switch" here. We do not offer grace at first and then judgment later. We offer grace to get people in the door and to keep them growing in the warmth of God's love. This grace is offered throughout a person's life and spiritual journey.

Graciousness

In the world of business, "distributors" are companies that sell products that other companies manufacture. In the church, we are not in the business of manufacturing grace. Grace has already been established through the life, death, and resurrection of Jesus Christ. The role of the church, quite simply, is to distribute this grace to others. We are in the business of helping people see and understand how significant God's grace can be for their lives, their churches, and the world. Churches would become more effective at this if they began thinking of themselves as distribution centers for God's grace.

In the fellowship of Alcoholics Anonymous, if a member slips and begins drinking again, everyone feels bad and hopes and prays that this person will find his or her way back into recovery and the fellowship of their community once again. When Christians slip, make mistakes, or sin, many insiders worry about how this will affect their churches. Or some worry that too much graciousness will encourage a sinful person to sin again. We wonder where we should draw the line. We wonder about leverage. We worry about what other people will think, particularly the people in our churches. We worry about the wrong things, at the wrong times, for the wrong reasons. Mike Yaconelli argues that God's grace is "ridiculously inclusive," but in the church today we tend to be embarrassingly exclusive.[1] In the church we often embrace law before grace, judgment before forgiveness, and intolerance before tolerance.

Grace does not give us a "blank check" to sin. Instead, grace changes us from the inside out. Grace does not just call us into the church; it also encourages us to be the church. Grace is the glue that holds the church together. It is the foundation of Christian hope and the springboard for Christian action. At Salem Covenant Church, our goal of encouraging openness and graciousness has been greatly assisted by several images. In his book *The Ragamuffin Gospel,* Brennan Manning quotes Morton Kelsey saying, "The church is not a museum for saints but a hospital for sinners."[2] I have used this quote over and over again to help nurture an "I'm not okay, you're not okay" approach within our congregation.

Hospitals are busy places filled with a great deal of activity surrounding sick and hurting people. Physician assistants, surgeons, nurses, receptionists, chaplains, administrators, food service providers, and social workers exist alongside primary care doctors. Hospitals house intensive care units, gift shops, cardiac care units, cafeterias, cancer centers, chapels, birthing centers, laundry rooms, operating rooms, kitchens, and medical floors. The level and variety of activities in hospitals are reflective of how things ought to be in our churches. There should be a lot of activity in our churches all focused primarily on those who are sick and hurting. We read in Luke 5:30–32: "The Pharisees and their scribes were complaining to his disciples, saying, 'Why do you eat and drink with tax collectors and sinners?' Jesus answered, 'Those who are well have no need of a physician, but those who are sick; I have come to call not the righteous but sinners to repentance.'"

Jesus, the great physician, reveals that the church exists to help broken people to begin putting their lives back together. In this way the church may be even more like a halfway house for those in need of redemption. Halfway houses exist to help people transition from mental hospitals, prisons, psychiatric wards, or drug treatment centers back into society. These homes provide a safe, supportive environment for individuals as they seek to transition into a new way of life. Churches should be safe places where sinful and broken people are supported as they seek to rebuild their lives and enter into the way of life that Jesus Christ has established for all of us.

It is not enough to talk about grace: we need to trust it. People need to see grace in action. They need to see Christian people living graciously and churches embracing grace-based policies and procedures. Living graciously allows us to say yes to Jesus and to the grace he offers. The church needs to move from guilt-based ministries to grace-based ministries that set people free from destructive levels of shame and allow them to freely live the kind of lives God always intended. Ultimately,

God wants us to be distributors of grace not judgment. This is why I advise churches to take an "I'm not okay, you're not okay" approach to being the church. This way we can freely welcome everyone in light of the fact that Jesus excluded no one.

Action Step #1

To develop an "I'm not okay, you're not okay" approach to being the church, a church must take several steps to change. The first step in any transformational process is evaluation. First, consider the direct and indirect messages your church sends out to others in the community. Where would your church be on the continuum below?

I'm okay,   I'm not okay,   I'm okay,
you're okay.   you're not okay.   you're not okay.

Where is your church now? Where do you want your church to be in the future? Is God calling your church to become an "honest to God church," where you will embrace the "I'm not okay, you're not okay" approach? To become a distribution center for God's grace and a halfway house for those being redeemed, we must embrace a grace-based approach to ministry. If the goal is transformation, then pastors, church leaders, and congregations must thoroughly evaluate their current situations and begin making changes that will help them move in this new direction. Please note that a move toward the "I'm not okay, you're not okay" approach is a move away from the extremes on the right and the left.

Discussion Questions

1. What is God's grace?
2. What is the difference between grace and graciousness?
3. Can you recall a time in your life when you have experienced grace or graciousness from another person? Please share about your experience.
4. Why is it important for those of us who have received grace from God to be willing to share it with others?
5. In what ways has the church been guilty of being the unforgiving servant in our generation?
6. What is the difference between tolerance and love? Which is better? Do you want others to tolerate you or love you?
7. What are the potential problems with an "I'm okay, you're not okay" approach to Christian ministry?
8. What are the potential problems with an "I'm okay, you're okay" approach to Christian ministry?
9. What are the potential strengths of the "I'm not okay, you're not okay" approach?
10. How do you think taking this approach more definitively would impact your church?
11. Do you think your church would benefit from seeing itself as a distribution center for grace, a hospital for sinners, or a halfway house for those in need of redemption? Talk about the strengths of each of these metaphors for the church.

Two

The Nice Church

W*hile I was a seminary student at North Park Theological* Seminary in Chicago, my wife and I also served as residence hall directors at North Park University, a small Christian college affiliated with the seminary. During this time, I met a student who often wore a sweatshirt around campus with a picture of his home church printed on it. I would laugh every time I saw him wearing this sweatshirt, because the name of his church was The Nice Church. No kidding, they called themselves The Nice Church! Were they implying that the "mean church" was down the street? Although I laughed every time I saw this sweatshirt, I also wanted to cry. Christian churches like to consider themselves friendly and nice, but Jesus did not die on the cross so we could be nice. Christianity ought to be about so much more than this. The church would have ceased to exist long ago if being nice was its only foundation.

Mystery

Jesus died so our sins could be forgiven and so we could freely live for things like righteousness, justice, and peace. There is nothing wrong with being nice. But being nice is not enough to allow us to call ourselves disciples or to call other people into a life of discipleship. The most compelling aspects of our faith call us to become radically committed to something larger than ourselves. Jesus is mysterious, and he calls us to follow him into a life that is filled with mystery, adventure, and meaning. We are called to follow Jesus faithfully and passionately. Jesus calls us to pick up our crosses, not simply to have good manners. Christianity is about embracing Jesus's teachings and way of life.

Christians and churches that reduce Christianity to being nice and friendly miss the central theme of the gospel and fail to understand why God sent his Son into the world. These failures make it essential to distinguish between a bland form of moderate religion and a bold form of Christian discipleship. There is a radical difference between being nice to your friends and loving your enemies. Through his earthly ministry, Jesus not only called us to love those we like but even to love those we dislike. Albert Nolan refers to Jesus's ethic of love as a "loving solidarity with all of humanity."[1] Jesus calls us to love all people because we all are created in the image of God. A loving solidarity with all of humanity demands that we treat all people with a deep level of respect. Living in loving solidarity with all of humanity reminds us to love the last and the least among us. True disciples are called to love the last and least in our world first and foremost.

If we believe in the truth of Christianity, we have no reason to be tentative around the people we encounter in life. We are called to live out the gospel in relationships with real people who have real problems. We fail miserably if we insulate ourselves from the world and live sheltered, protected lives. Tolerance is not enough, yet intolerance is one of the most destructive forces in the church today. Intolerance has to do with disregarding people because of who they are or how they behave. Jesus loves people as they are, and he calls on us to love them in the same way. Jesus calls us to love people regardless of their life circumstances, not judge them.

Many people like to "test" the church. Some push social boundaries because they want to know if we can accept them as they are or if we expect them to change before they are welcome. During my first year of ministry, I visited a man from our church in the hospital. And upon visiting him, I met a young woman who was also visiting him. He introduced us to each other, explaining that I was the new minister at his church. The young woman then proceeded to use as many four-letter words as she possibly could throughout the rest of our conversation. Every other word began with an *f*. She was seeking to evoke a response from me. Our mutual friend was uncomfortable and unsure about what to say or do. I think he almost had another heart attack! I simply kept the conversation going. She was testing me to see if I could accept her as she was. I ignored her language and treated her with as much respect as I could. I have had a positive relationship with her ever since. Actually, we have become good friends. She still swears around me but not as much.

Meanness

Being nice is not enough, but being mean is not a good alternative. Christians today can be downright mean. Christians from the extreme right are often more concerned with winning arguments than they are with the teachings of Jesus. Evangelical theologian Dallas Willard reflects on how mean Christians can be, particularly to those in Christian leadership. "Christians are routinely taught by example and word that it is more important to be right than it is to be Christ-like. In fact, being right licenses you to be mean, and, indeed, requires you to be mean—righteously mean, of course. You must be hard on people who are wrong, and especially if they are in positions of Christian leadership."[2] The apostle Paul addresses this very issue in the context of a debate going on in the early church. He writes in 1 Corinthians 8:1, "Knowledge puffs up, but love builds up." As

Christians we are called to build each other up, not tear each other down. Christian love demands that we pay more attention to our relationships than our arguments.

While speaking to a group of Christians, I was asked if clergy were as supportive of my teachings about grace and graciousness as were laypeople. The question subtly insinuated that clergy were to blame for the lack of grace found in many of our churches. Most clergy I know desire to be more gracious but often find it difficult because mean-spirited Christians see acts of grace as symbolic of moral weakness. Such people take on the role of watchdogs in our congregations, seeking to point out any gaps between what they believe is right and what their pastors allow other people to "get away with." Most church members and pastors hate conflict and often try to appease these ungracious individuals by limiting the amount of grace they distribute.

This kind of mean-spiritedness is the last thing we should permit in our churches if we want them to become distribution centers for God's grace. Mean Christians usually have louder voices than gracious ones. Therefore, gracious Christians must learn how to speak up and advocate for grace in our congregations. They must support their pastors and help them be the gracious and loving people God wants them to be. Clergy need visible and overt support, as they are often significantly battered and bruised by mean-spirited Christians. Such support will give pastors permission to offer the kind of leadership that will allow congregations to extend more grace to others, yet pastors also need to be willing to stand up for grace on their own, with or without the support of others.

Mercy

A lawyer from the Pharisees once tried to test Jesus with the question, "What must I do to inherit eternal life?" Jesus turned the tables on the lawyer by asking, "What is written in the law?

What do you read there?" The lawyer responded by referring to the great commandments. Jesus told him he was correct and continued by sharing the parable of the good Samaritan (Luke 10:25–37).

In this story, a priest and Levite (both members of the religious elite) passed by a man who had been attacked and was in desperate need of help. Then along came a "good for nothing" Samaritan. I say this because Pharisees did not associate with Samaritans. Samaritans were filthy in the eyes of the religious elite. I often think the parable should be renamed the "No good, good Samaritan." Jesus says in Luke 10:33–34, "But a Samaritan while traveling came near him; and when he saw him, he was moved with pity. He went to him and bandaged his wounds, having poured oil and wine on them."

Moreover, the Samaritan took this injured man to an inn and had him taken care of at his expense. This "no good" Samaritan did the good and right thing in the eyes of God. In Luke 10:36–37 Jesus asks the lawyer, "'Which one of these three, do you think, was a neighbor to the man who fell into the hands of the robbers?' He said, 'The one who showed him mercy.'" The lawyer could not even bring himself to say, "The Samaritan." He had to describe the man's actions, saying, "The one who showed mercy." His prejudice set Jesus up to have the last word. Jesus says, "Go and do likewise." Go and show mercy. Go and distribute grace.

The parable of the "no good, good Samaritan" is not a mandate to do good deeds. It is a judgment on the prejudice, hypocrisy, and judgmental attitudes of the religious elite. When the lawyer asks Jesus, "Who is my neighbor?" Jesus changes the question to, "Who was the better neighbor?" The underlying question becomes, "Who is not your neighbor?" Jesus teaches us over and over again that no one is to be excluded from our Christian love.

The mean-spirited way some Christians live out their faith tends to keep people from experiencing the compassion and gentleness of Jesus through us. Paul writes in Philippians 4:5, "Let your gentleness be known to everyone." Jesus does not want people to associate Christianity with "nice people" or "mean people." He wants the world to associate Christianity with transformed people who are capable of revealing his compassion and gentleness. The mystery of Christ and the power of God's grace often draw people into church. However, it is the lack of mystery and the lack of grace in many of our churches that turn people away. We need to stop trying to be in control. The church will be in much better shape if we allow God to be in control and his grace to flow freely.

Action Step #2

At Salem Covenant Church, one of the concrete things we did to become more than just another nice church was to develop a bold inclusive statement of welcome for our worship bulletin. It states:

> Visitors, we want to welcome you and say we are glad you are here. One of our goals here at Salem Covenant Church is to create an environment where all people feel loved and accepted by each other so we can, in turn, gain a clearer understanding of ourselves and our God.

This welcome statement had a much bigger impact on our church than I ever anticipated. After fourteen years, I have discovered that our church has truly embraced this as a goal. The welcome statement is often referred to in discussions at our church council meetings. One person told me that the statement is the reason he joined our church. Another person informed me that she reads it every Sunday morning. Quite surprisingly, our welcome statement has had a stronger impact on our congregation than our mission statement, vision statement, or any other leadership statement we have drafted.

If your congregation's goal is to become an "honest to God church," you should write a welcome statement for your church that is more than just polite. Develop a welcome statement that is gracious and inclusive of all people. Make sure this statement challenges your people to a loving solidarity with all of humanity. Make sure it allows the mystery of Christ to unfold and that it calls on your congregation to be more than just nice. Have your congregation approve the welcome statement at a congregational meeting. Then unveil your new statement to everyone and keep it in front of your people. Make sure your new welcome statement is in your bulletin every Sunday morning, and that it is front and center on the home page of your church website.

Discussion Questions

1. Why do you think a church might feel tempted to name itself "the nice church"?
2. What are some of the things churches should be committed to that help them to be more than just nice?
3. What did the apostle Paul mean when he said, "Knowledge puffs up, but love builds up"?
4. Why do some Christians think it is more important to be right than to be Christlike?
5. Have you ever been tested by anyone outside the church? Please share about your experiences.
6. What is wrong with intolerance?
7. What does it mean to live in loving solidarity with all of humanity?
8. Do you agree with Albert Nolan that a loving solidarity with all of humanity is Jesus' ethic? Why or why not?
9. How might embracing a loving solidarity with all of humanity help us to develop more honest to God churches?
10. Why might it make sense to rename the parable the "no good, good Samaritan"?
11. How might a church's preoccupation with being nice and friendly keep it from embracing the mystery of Christ?

Three

Radical Not Fanatical

*T*wo clearly defined groups of students coexisted on the relatively small Christian campus of North Park University during my years there as a residence hall director. There were those who went to chapel and Bible studies during their free time and those who preferred going to parties and bars. Occasionally there was some intermingling between the groups, but for the most part, the groups remained isolated from each other. The latter group was known as "the partiers."

At the end of one of the worst behavioral years on campus, one of the "partiers" came to me and shared that she felt one of the problems was that there was little if anything for the "partiers" to do spiritually on campus. I suggested that anyone on campus could attend the chapel services, campus ministry events, Bible studies, and other small groups. She said that the "partiers" did not feel welcome. Instead of arguing with her, I asked if she wanted to start a new group just for the partiers. She responded enthusiastically. She said that if I would lead it, she would get the group together. I readily agreed to this plan. At our first meeting in the fall, she assembled what appeared, on the surface, to be the twelve least likely candidates from our campus to be in a Bible study.

That year we had one of the best Bible studies I have ever led. We met every week all year. No one ever had to be reminded to come. When I asked if they wanted to take a break during finals week, everybody responded, "No!" The young woman who helped me start this group later referred to our Bible study as "egg carton evangelism." She said that I was willing to take them all in and give them a safe place to learn and grow spiritually. In reality, all I did was show up and enjoy the astonishingly spiritual discussions we had about God, life, Jesus, the church, the Bible, and our world.

Evangelism

After graduating from North Park University, this young woman went on to North Park Theological Seminary and graduated with a master of divinity degree. For her seminary internship, she spent a year walking across America to learn more about discipleship and evangelism. She then went on to travel around the country speaking at church camps, Christian conferences, and youth retreats. She has become one of the most respected conference speakers in our denomination. Ironically, she was recently called to be the chaplain at North Park University—the same Christian school where this egg carton evangelism took place. The good news is that the one who did not feel welcome in the chapel is now the chaplain.

Too often we in the church turn people away who need to be held tightly. Lack of trust in grace leads many congregations to become rigid and judgmental rather than loving and flexible. Our membership practices and policies lead us to exclude people before we have given them a chance to be exposed to God's grace, let alone embraced by it. We take God's almighty grace, put it in a box, place it on a shelf, and fail to allow its power into our lives and into the lives of others.

A good friend of mine has a grown-up daughter who refuses to consider Christianity as a viable option for her life. She views Christianity as closed, restrictive, narrow, exclusive, and shallow. She argues that Christians and Christianity have failed to meet her spiritual needs and the spiritual needs of our nation and world. Christianity, she feels, has been given its chance and failed miserably. She sees Christianity as irrelevant to her life and spiritual journey, and she is not alone. Many people have a tarnished image of Christianity because of its mistakes and failure to be honest about them. Many teachings in churches today have little to do with Jesus. Jesus embodied grace. Jesus was not shallow, close-minded, or exclusive in his approach to ministry. Rather, his ministry was deep, open, wide, and inclusive. I am convinced that an honest to God approach is the only way we will be able to get back to an authentic form of Christian discipleship where these realities can be brought back to life in our congregations.

Fanaticism

Christians who appear seriously committed to their faith fall into two groups: fanatical and radical Christians. Many people in churches today are afraid to take their faith seriously because subconsciously they fear becoming religious fanatics. Fanatics tend to be the most visible people among those who consider themselves committed Christians. They are the ones who are more interested in winning arguments than maintaining relationships. The gentleness and humility that Jesus embraced often escape them. At times I wonder how many people are turned away from Christianity by fanaticism. Fanatical Christians occasionally connect with people, but they turn off countless more.

Fanatical Christians take their faith seriously—but only from the neck up. In reality, they take themselves more seriously than the faith. Fanatics are often self-centered, self-serving, and self-absorbed. Radical Christians take their faith seriously but also remain committed and concerned for those around them.

Fanatical Christians tend to be judgmental, whereas radical Christians tend to be compassionate. Fanatical Christians focus on governing the moral lives of others, whereas radical Christians seek justice and offer practical support to those who need it most. In his book *Following Jesus without Embarrassing God,* Tony Campolo writes, "It's one thing for the world to reject Jesus because the people in secular society consider the gospel ridiculous. It is quite another thing for the world to reject the gospel because Christians are an embarrassment to God."[1]

One of the reasons many people choose fanatical Christianity is because it is easier than radical Christianity. The fast pace of our lives leaves little time for us, let alone for God and others. If our faith exists only "from the neck up," we only have to be concerned about committing ourselves to a few ideas and rules. Radical Christianity demands that we commit ourselves to one another, not just to a set of clearly defined positions. To become radical Christians, we must be concerned with the whole of people's lives, not just with what they believe. To become radical Christians, we must move away from the extremes of the right and the left to discover a more balanced and committed alternative.

Radical Christianity

Radical Christians recognize that there is a gap between the way things are in our world and the way things ought to be. They seek to help meet the physical, emotional, and spiritual needs of others. They emphasize caring for the whole person. Fanatical Christians concern themselves only with what people are thinking, though ironically they usually don't want people to think too much. Fanatical Christianity leaves little room for wonder and questioning. A fanatic's fear of the unknown is often more powerful than the desire to embrace the Christian faith and

God's grace with any clear sense of assurance or integrity. For fanatics, the Christian faith resembles a house of cards ready to fall at any moment. Radical Christians see the Christian faith as a strong foundation for their lives. They acknowledge the mystery of Christ and seek to live in it.

Radical Christians recognize the power of God and are humbled. They are not defensive about their beliefs or afraid to tackle the difficult questions people ask about God and this world. Honest faith always has an element of doubt in it. Mature Christians recognize this and embrace the mystery. Hebrews 11:1 says, "Faith is the assurance of things hoped for, the conviction of things not seen." Sharing one's faith isn't about forcing others to believe everything you believe. Rather, it is about living in the midst of God's grace and sharing his love for the world with others.

Radical commitments to Christ make Christianity more palatable to nonbelievers. Radical commitments to Christ make it possible to spread the good news of God's grace more effectively. Radical Christians care about the spiritual and practical needs of others. They care about individuals, nations, and the world. They care about everything and everyone that would be of concern to Jesus if he were living on the earth among us today. No one ever said that following Jesus would be easy. Being a committed Christian takes time and energy.

Fanatical Christianity represents a detour many people have taken off the road of true Christian discipleship. We should all be concerned and uneasy with the stranglehold many fanatics have on Christianity today. A productive response to fanaticism must be centered on developing radical commitments in our own lives as we recognize that taking one's faith seriously does not lead to fanaticism. A person does not become a radical Christian the first time they make a radical commitment, but as those commitments accumulate, we become more and more radically committed to the faith. Both religious fanatics and radical Christians can be found in all denominations and churches. The problem is that there are too many fanatics and not enough devoted disciples.

The fruit of the Spirit described in Galatians 5:22–23 reveals the kind of lives God wants us to live: "The fruit of the Spirit is love, joy, peace, patience, kindness, generosity, faithfulness, gentleness, and self-control." Fruits of the Spirit are virtues that grow out of our lives when the Spirit of God is at work within us and we are paying attention to the things that matter most to God. We are not to pretend to have these virtues, for God does not want fake fruit that looks real but lacks substance. God calls us to grow real fruit as a result of the real work the Holy Spirit does in us. Tending to the needs of the soul is tending to the soil in which this fruit can grow. God gives the growth, but we can prepare the soil and tend to the garden within us to help these virtues begin to flourish. In the parable of the sower, Jesus compares good soil to those who hold God's word in an "honest and good heart" (Luke 8:15).

The extremes on the right and the left appeal to people because time is a huge hurdle for radical Christianity. Day-to-day work obligations, household chores, and family activities sap most of our time. Time is finite, and it is easy for ordinary activities to keep us from making extraordinary commitments. But if we want a meaningful life, we have to do meaningful things. If we want the church to be what God wants it to be, we need to be a part of the solution not the problem. We should not allow our lack of time to lead us into embracing a shallow or distorted view of Christianity. We must avoid this and cultivate honest hearts that are committed to the things Jesus desires.

Action Step #3

At Salem Covenant Church, we are doing more to help the people in our community and region than ever before, but we could still do more. Our church prepares and serves a meal once a month at a local soup kitchen. We have participated in several Habitat for Humanity projects. Many in our congregation have volunteered by driving for Meals on Wheels, tutoring people who are learning English as a second language, transporting homebound people to doctor appointments, and visiting those who are sick and suffering. One member has been actively involved in a local Big Brother/Big Sister Program. We also commit ourselves to support a variety of service organizations with our mission budget, including a women's shelter and the Boys and Girls Club in our community. Further, we have developed a connection with World Relief and Bread for the World. These things are by no means extraordinary, but they are the kind of commitments that can help us to embrace a more radical form of Christianity. These kinds of commitments, combined with a more open and inclusive approach to ministry, have truly helped us become a more grace-based congregation.

In the process of becoming an honest to God church, work with your church leaders to develop a short list of commitments your church members could make in your community and region. You may actually want to make two lists—one for radical commitments your church could make as a group and the second for radical commitments individuals from your church could pursue on their own. Serving at homeless shelters or soup kitchens, tutoring people learning English, working with Habitat for Humanity, developing a babysitting ministry to support single parents, creating health-care ministries, and writing letters to politicians on behalf of the poor are all examples of the type of radical commitments your church may want to include on their to-do lists. The focus should always be on progress, not perfection. We do not become radical congregations over night, yet we should not allow ordinary things to keep us from pursuing the extraordinary goal of faithfully following Jesus. The goal is not to become a perfect church; it is to let God's perfect love inspire us to do good things for others.

Discussion Questions

1. What is the difference between radical and fanatical Christianity?
2. Have you ever had a bad experience with a fanatical Christian? Talk about your experience.
3. Why do some people in our society have a hard time with Christianity, yet they do not struggle with Jesus?
4. Why does the fear of becoming a fanatic keep some people from taking their faith seriously?
5. Why is it important to take our Christian faith seriously?
6. Why is being a radical Christian harder than being a fanatical Christian?
7. Do you know any radical Christians? Describe them.
8. What makes radical commitments worthwhile for the church?
9. What are some of the things you do in your life that make it meaningful?
10. What are some of the radical commitments your church has made in the past? What are some that it could make in the future?
11. What is the difference between the real fruit of the Spirit and fake fruit?
12. What kind of message do our radical commitments make to our world about the church and Christianity?

Four

Passion and Compassion

I *was once asked by a person familiar with my position on* grace what I would do if an unmarried couple living together wanted to join my church. Ironically, I was dealing with such a situation in real life at that time. The couple I knew lived together while both were in the process of finalizing painful and complicated divorces. They wanted to get married but couldn't. They came to our church out of pain, frustration, and chaos, seeking spiritual solutions to their problems. They needed God and the church at this critical time in their lives.

After several months, this couple expressed a tremendous appreciation for the love and acceptance they felt in our church. They clearly experienced grace and were embraced by it. Eventually, they joined our new member class. It was here that I faced the question of their living together. My philosophy on ministry had always been to be as gracious as I possibly could with regard to these complicated life and church situations. I chose grace over judgment, and they happily joined our church. With time, they grew in their faith, married, and remained active members in our church.

It is worth noting that the woman in the couple is an accomplished artist. Her paintings are sold in prominent art galleries in New York City, Chicago, and Los Angeles. An art critic once described her paintings as being reminiscent of the Garden of Eden. One Saturday evening while at an opening in New York City, a friend asked if she would like to go out and get a drink afterward. She responded by saying that she could not because she had to return home to prepare for teaching Sunday school the next morning. Her friend's jaw dropped. My friend surprised her friend by being committed to the church in a way that most of her contemporaries in the art world have not been. The good news is that grace breaks down barriers and brings people into our churches that otherwise might not be there.

Passion

Jesus was a passionate leader. He turned over tables. He ate with sinners and tax collectors. He touched lepers. He confronted the chief priests and Pharisees. He healed the sick, cured the blind, and raised people from the dead. He walked on water, fed five thousand people with two loaves of bread and three fish, turned water into wine, prayed regularly, and washed the feet of his disciples. He was tested, arrested, convicted, and crucified by the religious elite of his day primarily because his passion attracted too much attention. He touched the untouchable and loved the unlovable.

Passion embodies enthusiasm, excitement, and exuberance. It is the driving force in our lives that energizes us and keeps us focused. Some people are passionate about sports; others, art or music. For some, their passion is working, making money, or achieving personal success. Still others are passionate about relationships, romance, or friendships. As Christians, we should seek to become more passionate about the relationships we have with God and one another. Our passion should lead us to follow Jesus and to help others follow him as well. Our passion should be for loving God and loving our neighbors as fully and faithfully as we possibly can. Our passion should not be to prove how conservative or liberal we are, but rather to show how kind and compassionate we can be.

The first few years after I accepted Jesus into my life were filled with passion. I was a high school student thrilled to have encountered Jesus in a personal way. I read my Bible and met with other Christians regularly. I was actively involved with prayer and ministry. I sought out every opportunity I could to tell people about Jesus and his impact on my life. I felt like my faith would grow forever, and I had a hard time understanding people who talked about backsliding or losing passion in their faith. I experienced a honeymoon period with regard to my faith—an uninterrupted time of getting to know Jesus and letting Jesus get to know me.

After some time in my own spiritual journey, I came to question how to sustain my faith and enthusiasm. My walk with God began like a blazing fire but eventually turned to smoldering coals. How does one keep the fire of faith burning? I came to discover a clear connection between passion and compassion. Compassion helps us to keep our spiritual lives alive and vital. Passion without compassion is like a candle with a very short wick: it inevitably fizzles out, and rightfully so. Faith is not a selfish, self-centered commodity. It is not something we possess, but rather something that possesses us. I believe this connection between passion and compassion is a part of God's plan for keeping the church and our spiritual lives from digressing into religious sentimentalism. Compassion is the pain we feel for others who suffer. It is both sympathetic and empathetic, and it calls on us to be real and to have true concern for the issues people face in life.

Compassion

To take our faith seriously, we must take the compassion of Jesus seriously. Jesus not only taught us to be passionate about spiritual things, but also to be compassionate about the physical and emotional needs of others. It is by facing life's difficulties together that we overcome the distractions that keep us divided. Only compassion can keep the community of the church united and passionate about serving in our world. The passion of Jesus was intensified by the compassion he had for others. Compassion is what led Jesus to heal, pray, and forgive. Compassion motivated him to preach, lead, and teach. Compassion enabled him to endure the pain and death of the cross on our behalf. His passion was motivated and fueled by compassion.

Compassion leads us to care about others, and it enables us to become Christ-centered followers of Jesus. In his book *Jesus Before Christianity*, Albert Nolan writes, "We do not need to theorize about Jesus, we need to 're-produce' him in our time and our circumstances. He himself did not regard the truth as something we simply 'uphold' and 'maintain,' but as something we choose to live and experience."[1]

Human beings have a strong disposition toward self-centeredness. Christians often lack spiritual direction because we focus only on our selfish concerns and desires. We concern ourselves more with what God can do for us than on what we can do for God. We must begin to think beyond ourselves to reclaim the passion that is so elusive in the church today. To be both self-centered and Christ-centered simultaneously is impossible. We need to become more Christ-centered in our discipleship and our churches.

Sacrifice

The word passion is related to the word suffering. When Christian scholars refer to the "passion narratives," they are talking about the stories of Jesus's suffering that ended on the cross. The root Latin word *passio* means to suffer. This is why Mel Gibson named his epic movie about Christ's suffering and death

The Passion of the Christ. Passion and suffering often go hand in hand. Sacrifice has to do with believing in something so passionately you are willing to surrender your life for the cause. It is this kind of passion that cannot exist appropriately without compassion.

Much has been said historically about the Christian church's failure to stand up to Nazi Germany. Dietrich Bonhoffer was a Christian theologian who wrote from the perspective of being a committed Christian in Nazi Germany during the rise and fall of Adolf Hitler. Bonhoffer was imprisoned in a concentration camp during World War II for his beliefs. Few would argue that Bonhoffer was a religious fanatic. Rather, his actions demonstrate a radical commitment to Christ. In his book *The Cost of Discipleship,* Bonhoffer advocates self-denial. He writes, "To deny oneself is to be aware only of Christ and no more of self, to see only him who goes before and no more the road which is too hard for us."[2] As Christians we are at times called to choose the more difficult path. We cannot be compassionate Christians and always chose the path of least resistance. Short term, the more difficult path may demand more of us, but in the long run, it will lead us toward a better and brighter future.

The idea of sacrifice is difficult for many of us because we have significant pain in our lives already. Our pain and suffering leave us feeling overwhelmed and keep us preoccupied with ourselves. The idea of choosing suffering seems ludicrous, yet according to Jesus, we must practice self-sacrifice if we hope to become his true disciples. True disciples are called to pick up their crosses and follow him. Ironically, choosing self-sacrifice and suffering can set us free from preoccupation with ourselves and our pain.

Spiritual maturity does not mean a loss of passion. Spiritual maturity means coming to a point in your spiritual journey where you discover the connection between passion and compassion. Spiritual maturity means gaining insight into the relationships that exist between things like faith and faithfulness and grace and graciousness. Spiritually mature Christians can be even more passionate about their faith than new Christians if they understand these connections. God does not want us to receive his love and grace only to keep them for ourselves. He wants us to share them continually with others. We are called not only to embrace God's grace, but also to convey it through all we say and do.

Action Step #4

There is a trend in evangelism today that recognizes the need people have to belong before they will believe. They have to join a Christian community before they will open up to personal faith. This is ironic, because most churches require belief before belonging. We expect people to confess the Christian faith before they can officially join our congregations. In many ways we expect people to be finished before they really get started. Our membership policies and practices do not allow much room for the mysterious mix of believing, belonging, and becoming that are required for spiritual growth. Discipleship is a lifelong journey, not a line that we need to jump across. Our membership policies and practices should allow people to come as they are and to grow over time. We need to develop policies and practices that allow our churches to be compassionate toward the broken people who come to us for help.

At Salem Covenant Church we are obligated to follow our denomination's expectation of believing before belonging. However, in our new member classes, we discuss how becoming a church member is a starting point, not a finish line. Joining the church is the beginning of a journey in which people grow spiritually over time. This is why I also teach about what it means to be in an "I'm not okay, you're not okay" church, which encourages spiritual growth at every point along our faith journey. On an airplane recently, a gentleman shared with me his church's motto: "No perfect people allowed." I have used this story and statement ever since.

Honest to God churches must create membership policies and practices that encourage current members to show compassion to the broken people entering our churches. Failure to do so will mean your membership will grow only if traditional Christians come to your church after leaving other congregations. Inviting people who are struggling with life can be a wonderful blessing for your congregation. Love should always be at the center of our identity as Christians, and offering grace graciously is one of the primary ways we can love the people who come into our churches seeking help for their lives.

Discussion Questions

1. What is the difference between passion and compassion?
2. Why is passion important?
3. How does compassion help us to keep our passion alive?
4. What is dangerous about having passion without compassion?
5. In what ways was Jesus a passionate and/or a compassionate leader?
6. What do you find most inspiring for your life, Jesus's passion or his compassion?
7. What are our churches lacking more of—compassion or passion?
8. Can churches reclaim passion without compassion?
9. Why is the concept of sacrifice difficult for many of us?
10. What are some ways you deal with suffering in your life?
11. What is spiritual maturity?
12. Why is it important for churches to see church membership as a starting point rather than a finish line?

Five

Entitlement and Nullification

W*hile visiting a member of my church in her home, I entered* into a conversation with her son-in-law who claimed to be an atheist. When he told me that he was an atheist, I responded in the way I usually do, saying, "I do not believe in atheists." He quickly responded, "Just because you say that you do not believe in something does not mean that it is not real." After he said this, he realized that he had backed himself into a corner. I said, "That is my point exactly." We both laughed.

I think a lot of people who claim to be atheists are really just distancing themselves from God because they do not want to confront the spiritual side of their lives. They do not want to deal with God or themselves. They utilize their claim to be atheists as a way of avoiding God and the difficult issues in their lives. Often it is in the face of grave danger or life-challenging circumstances that these people acknowledge God and begin to deal with the issues they had been trying to avoid.

Self-Deception

Over the past several decades, many Christians and Christian churches have bought into secular rather than theological explanations for our world's most pressing problems. Low self-esteem was the primary concern of most mental health professionals during the 1970s and '80s. This led many churches to become more interested in self-help than the help God could offer. Many mainline churches did book studies in the 1970s on the grandparent of all self-help books, *I'm OK—You're OK* by Thomas Harris. Ever since this book was written, people have been frantically trying to convince themselves that they're okay even when they're not. The strange thing is that deep down we all know we're not perfect, and we inherently understand that our churches and our world aren't either. Yet we frantically try to convince ourselves otherwise. This is called self-deception.

Intentionally or not, the self-esteem movement led many people in our culture to teach children to think about themselves as being better than everyone else around them. Now psychologists and other mental health professionals are even more concerned with what they are calling "entitlement issues." They see young people on a regular basis who are absolutely certain their lives should be better than they are and that someone else is to blame. Our approach to addressing self-esteem issues has left many with an overblown sense of entitlement and has led to a culture of blame and complaining in our society. Many people today have difficulty dealing with normal disappointments and typical life challenges. They are too easily offended, and they do not accept enough personal responsibility.

My ultimate fear is that these entitlement issues are not only impacting the way people relate to each other, but also how we relate to God. If we do not acknowledge our problems, then we fail to acknowledge our need for God and God's people. Proverbs 9:10 says, "The fear of the LORD is the beginning of wisdom." Our culture does not encourage us to fear and respect God. While many in the United States say they believe in God, most live like atheists by failing to give much if any attention to the difference between right and wrong. In "I'm okay, you're okay" churches, people live under the illusion that there is no difference between right and wrong and that they do not need God's grace.

Heaven

A few years ago, *Time* magazine put on its cover a picture of a man standing on a single cloud in front of a blue sky looking outward. The caption with this image read, "Does Heaven Exist?"[1] The article gave the impression that most people in our society believe heaven exists and that they will go there when they die regardless of their beliefs or behavior. My fear is that too many people have a false sense of entitlement with regard to heaven. They feel that life is not all it is cracked up to be and that God owes them one. Many believe they will get into heaven because they are entitled to it, not because of anything they have done for God or that God has done for them. Many people no longer think about heaven as a gift, but rather as a consolation prize.

When children expect certain gifts on Christmas or birthdays, their gratitude for such gifts is often replaced by a sense of entitlement that takes all the fun out of gift giving. Many children want more than they receive, which typically keeps them from appreciating what they are given. People who see heaven as a consolation prize are like these children in that they place so much emphasis on what they expect, that they fail to appreciate the gift being offered. These people play up the idea that they have been victimized by life. They go on about how their lives have not been enjoyable and how they feel that they should be fairly compensated in heaven for all they have had to endure while here on earth. They blame God for what they have not received in life.

People with a strong sense of entitlement are typically not very resilient. Dr. Kathleen Brehony, a psychotherapist, author, and personal coach, writes, "Resilience implies a kind of toughness and flexibility that harbors the power to recover. It is elasticity in the face of pain and suffering. To me the word also conjures up optimism, perseverance, and resourcefulness."[2] One of the most resilient people I know is a good friend of mine who is a recovering alcoholic. He has been a sober member of Alcoholics Anonymous for more than twenty-five years. He also recently went through a serious battle with cancer, and instead of saying, "Why me?" he asked, "Why not me?" or "Why anyone?" To develop resilience and avoid entitlement, we must stop thinking about what God has failed to do for us and start thinking about what we have failed to do for God. Life is not always easy, but God never promised it would be. We must face a certain amount of challenge in life with God's help and the help of others around us, because this is how God designed our world to work. God wants us to admit that we need him and one another.

Nullification

My primary concern with those who see heaven as a consolation prize relates to something the apostle Paul points toward as the "nullification" of God's grace. Paul writes in Galatians 2:15–21 about justification by grace in the context of the debate over the Jew and Gentile division that existed within the early church. The question back then was related to whether Gentiles had to follow Jewish law to be justified by faith in Jesus. In the last few verses of this passage, Paul says, "I have been crucified with Christ; and it is no longer I who live, but it is Christ who lives in me. And the life I now live in the flesh I live by faith in the Son of God; who loved me and gave himself for me. I do not nullify the grace of God; for if justification comes through the law, then Christ died for nothing." These were strong words, spoken about a very specific and significant problem in the early church. And in our day this matter of nullification is relevant to the issues I raise here. If people falsely believe they are going to heaven because God owes them one—because they are entitled to it—they may very well be nullifying God's grace. They may inadvertently be saying that Christ died for nothing.

God's grace must be acknowledged above all else as necessary. We must develop a proper understanding of who we are as human beings and what we need from God. What we need is God's grace, but we must recognize that the gift of grace is not a payment for services rendered or a consolation prize for those of us who experience pain and suffering. Jesus paid for our sins on the cross. Salvation is a gift, not something we earn or even deserve. God gives us this gift because he loves us. He offers it to us because he created us in his image. He wants us to have it because we are his children.

God also cares deeply about our pain and suffering, and the gift of heaven is as much related to our pain as it is to our sin. In fact, the Beatitudes reveal that God may offer the gift of heaven first and foremost to those who have endured the most suffering among us. The first three beatitudes say, "Blessed are the poor in spirit, for theirs is the kingdom of heaven. Blessed are those who mourn, for they will be comforted. Blessed are the meek, for they will inherit the earth" (Matt. 5:3–5).

Most modern Christians do not think about the Beatitudes in terms of who will go to heaven. But maybe we should. Maybe we should think about how God's grace is first and foremost for those who experience the most pain among us and how the promise of God's kingdom comes to them first. It would not surprise me to discover that some people get into heaven simply by the compassion God feels toward them because of the *extreme* pain they have endured in their lives. Having said that, let me also say that pain is a normal part of all our lives, and we should not expect to get into heaven simply because we experience it.

God does not want us to go through life angry because things don't always go our way. He certainly does not want us to feel as if we deserve heaven because of the moderate levels of pain most of us experience in life. If we believe we are entitled to the gifts we receive from God, they are no longer gifts at all. If we allow pain and entitlement to keep us from a loving relationship with God, we may not only miss out on God's grace in the here and now, but also in the hereafter. We have to see God's grace as a gift, not as a consolation prize, if we hope to embrace it completely within our lives.

Action Step #5

One of the ways my denomination defines *evangelism* is anything we say or do that helps another person move one step closer to Jesus. God is a big part of people's lives whether they realize it or not. By offering God's grace to people in our world through a commitment to evangelism, we reveal that we see the need all people have for Jesus. Yet through our evangelism, we must emphasize that we are not perfect but that God helps us with our imperfections, sins, and brokenness. God helps us to deal with the fact that we are not okay, and that we will never be completely okay until we get to heaven. If honest to God churches take God's grace seriously, they will seriously reach out and evangelize, helping those around them to move closer to God.

Once a year at Salem Covenant Church we encourage our church members to write down the names of people they want to help move one step closer to Jesus. Our denomination calls this "Bringing My World to Christ Sunday." If we believe all people need God's grace, it is our job to help them to discover it. In your quest to develop honest to God churches, I would encourage you to develop a "Bringing My World to Christ Sunday" for your church. Encouraging your church members to prepare a list of names for themselves is a great way to get them to focus on evangelism. And urging them to pray for the people on their lists throughout the year will keep them thinking about evangelism. Churches should always encourage their members to ask God to use them as instruments to help move others closer to Jesus.

Discussion Questions

1. What do helping professionals mean when they refer to low self-esteem?
2. What have helping professionals seen as the answer to low self-esteem over the past several decades?
3. What do helping professionals mean when they say that a person has developed a sense of entitlement?
4. How has the self-esteem movement contributed to the high sense of entitlement many people feel today?
5. Why do some people in our society feel entitled to go to heaven?
6. What is the difference between seeing heaven as a gift and seeing heaven as a consolation prize?
7. In what ways do we take God and his grace for granted?
8. Why does our pain sometimes keep us from seeing God's grace as a gift?
9. How might it help people to stop asking, "Why me?" when they are sick or suffering and instead to ask, "Why not me?" or "Why anyone?"
10. How might it help people to stop asking God what he has done for them lately and start asking what they have done for God lately?
11. If heaven is a gift, not a consolation prize, then how important is evangelism? What do you think about defining evangelism as helping others to move one step closer to Jesus?

Six

Pain and Redemption

*O*nce while visiting New York City, my wife and I spent some time at St. Patrick's Cathedral. Inside this majestic place there stands an intriguing life-size marble sculpture of Mary holding the adult Jesus in her arms after the crucifixion. This image of Mary cradling Jesus is called a *pietà*. While I was standing there looking at this pietà, a well-dressed woman walked confidently into the sanctuary holding a briefcase. She had on a red business suit and looked as if she fit well in the fast-paced New York City corporate environment. She looked like someone who had it all together, who could handle just about anything life would throw at her. As she drew close to the statue, however, she put her hand on the edge of Jesus's clothing and fell to her knees and wept. As she reached out for Jesus' hand, this woman revealed her brokenness and began to cry profusely. She let go of all she held close and gave herself permission to be vulnerable with God no matter what anyone else around her was doing or thinking.

Pain

"Enough is enough" is a phrase often used by those overwhelmed by life's circumstances. Physical ailments, personal grief, relationship troubles, and occupational crises burden our lives and leave us feeling overwhelmed. In his second letter to the Corinthians, the apostle Paul referred to a "thorn" in his "flesh." Although we don't know the exact nature of the "thorn," we can assume Paul was referring to some type of physical ailment or limitation. Paul writes in 2 Corinthians 12:8–10:

> Three times I appealed to the Lord about this, that it would leave me, but he said to me, "My grace is sufficient for you, for power is made perfect in weakness." So, I will boast all the more gladly of my weakness, so that the power of Christ may dwell in me. Therefore I am content with weakness, insults, hardships, persecutions, and calamities for the sake of Christ; for whenever I am weak, then I am strong.

I find it difficult to imagine being content with "weakness, insults, hardships, persecutions, and calamities." Yet there is no evidence in the text that suggests that Paul enjoyed these realities. It simply says that he recognized that none of these painful realities could compare with the weight of the glory that comes to us from God's grace. Paul's ailments and struggles did not keep him from putting his complete trust in God. Paul understood that God's grace was sufficient for him.

One of the biggest challenges we all face in life is rising above our personal issues so we can live fully and faithfully for God. Life has a way of pulling us down and holding us back. Struggles with grief and pain can easily distract us. But the apostle Paul reveals that we can rise above our problems and live fully and faithfully for God if we trust in the sufficiency of God's grace. Doing so means we recognize that what God has already done for us through Christ Jesus is enough.

Although we may be discouraged when we ask God to take away pain and it remains, we will never be content with our life circumstances if we do not learn how to see God's grace as enough. If we focus on the sufficiency of God's grace rather than on the things we wish God was doing for us now, then enough will be enough in our minds, and this will help us to shape a more positive attitude for our futures. The real substance of the Christian faith is sufficient grace. It is the main course. Everything else God does for us is the gravy.

God wants us to appreciate the things he does for us on a regular basis, but above all else, God wants us to show him our greatest appreciation for what Jesus did on the cross. When Jesus breathed his last breath, the Bible tells us that the curtain separating people from the Holy of Holies in the temple was torn in two. The holiest place in the temple was thought to be so permeated by God's presence that no human being could enter it. Matthew 27:50–51 says, "Then Jesus cried again with a loud voice and breathed his last. At that moment the curtain of the temple was torn in two, from top to bottom. The earth shook, and the rocks were split." The curtain tore because Christ's death eliminated all that separates us from God. The tearing of the temple curtain clearly reveals the dynamic and powerful nature of God's grace.

Redemption

In *The Ragamuffin Gospel*, Brennan Manning confesses that he became an alcoholic after he became a Christian. People often asked him how that was possible. He responds, "I got battered and bruised by loneliness and failure, because I got discouraged, uncertain, guilt-ridden, and took my eyes off of Jesus." He writes, "There is a myth flourishing in the church today that has caused incalculable harm—once converted, fully converted. In other words, once I accept Jesus Christ as my Lord and Savior, an irreversible, sinless future beckons. Discipleship will be an untarnished success story; life will be an unbroken upward spiral toward holiness."[1]

The story of Peter's life and discipleship in the Bible reveals over and over again that discipleship is anything but an untarnished success story. Peter's experience shows that redemption is a process, not an event, and that significant transformation can take place long after we make the initial decision to follow Jesus. A conversion experience may mark the starting point in our relationship with Jesus, but mini conversion experiences allow us to continue to grow and be transformed over time throughout our spiritual journey.

According to John's Gospel, the final resurrection appearance Jesus made to his disciples was on the beach after they had been out on a boat fishing all night and caught nothing. Speaking from the beach, Jesus had them cast their nets out one more time. They followed his instructions, and their nets became full with fish, which was clearly reminiscent of the day Jesus initially called Peter to follow him. Jesus then welcomed them back to the beach with a hot fire and a warm breakfast. Jesus not only made the fire and prepared the food, but he also served the meal.

After they had finished eating, Jesus said to Simon Peter, "Simon son of John, do you love me more than these?" (John 21:15). This is an interesting question, for it reveals the uniqueness of the relationship Peter had with Jesus. He was the first one called to be a disciple and he was the disciple most often referred to by name in the gospel stories. Peter responded to Jesus's question, saying, "Yes, Lord; you know that I love you." Jesus said to him, "Feed my lambs." The conversation continues in verses 16–17:

> A second time he said to him, "Simon son of John, do you love me?" He said to him, "Yes Lord; you know that I love you." Jesus said to him, "Tend my sheep." He said to him the third time, "Simon son of John, do you love me?" Then Peter felt hurt because he said to him the third time, "Do you love me?" And he said to him, "Lord, you know everything; you know that I love you." Jesus said to him, "Feed my sheep."

The gentleness Jesus demonstrated on the beach that day began to wane as he asked Peter these repetitive questions. The warm food and fire revealed his gentleness, but Jesus also revealed firmness by asking Peter the same question three times until it hurt. Was it necessary for Jesus to make Peter hurt in this way? Why did Jesus have to keep pushing him?

The reason Jesus had to ask Peter this question three times has to do with the time just before Jesus's arrest when Peter promised Jesus he would stand by him and stand up for him no matter what happened. In John 13:36–38 Peter promised Jesus his loyalty and devotion.

> Simon Peter said to him, "Lord, where are you going?" Jesus answered, "Where I am going, you cannot follow me now; but you will follow me afterward." Peter said to him, "Lord, why can I not follow you now? I will lay down my life for you." Jesus answered, "Will you lay down your life for me? Very truly, I tell you, before the cock crows, you will have denied me three times."

Peter, in fact, proceeded to deny Jesus three times. And in the end, Peter did not lay down his life for Jesus; rather, Jesus laid down his life for Peter—and for every one of us. At first Peter did not realize that Jesus had to be the one to lay down his life. It was necessary for Jesus to do this alone, for he alone bore our sins in his body on the cross. He alone wore the crown of thorns and received the torment and torture of the crucifixion. He alone breathed his last breath and was laid in an empty tomb. He alone was raised from that grave.

Peter felt he had failed Jesus miserably. But the words Peter needed to remember were, "You cannot follow me now; but you will follow afterward." Peter was very important to Jesus. Jesus loved Peter, but Peter could not have gone to the cross in the same way Jesus did. Jesus had to do it alone. This is why Peter had to deny him, and this is why in the end Jesus wanted Peter to feel reconciled with him before his ascension. Peter's relationship with Jesus needed to be redeemed. As Peter said, Jesus knew everything, and he knew that Peter loved him, but he also knew that Peter felt bad about his actions and unsure about his role after denying him three times at the time he thought Jesus needed him the most. Therefore, Jesus knew that if he did not ask Peter if he loved him three times, Peter would have continued to carry an unbearable burden. Peter would have continued to feel guilty about denying him, and this would have increased his level of discouragement. He may have wondered whether he was worthy to continue serving Jesus.

This story reveals that pain will always be a part of our earthly lives, and that redemption is at times a painful process. When Jesus asked Peter three times, "Do you love me?" it hurt, and this may not have been particularly good for Peter's ego, but it was good for his soul. There are times in all of our lives when we fail to follow Jesus as we ought. In these times, we need to put ourselves in Peter's shoes and allow Jesus to ask us three times, "Do you love me?" We need to respond by saying, "Yes, Lord, you know that I love you." Then we need to hear Jesus say, "Feed my sheep." This process not only redeems, but it also calls us back into action. It may hurt, but it is still good for the soul. Repentance equips us for effective discipleship and ministry.

"I'm okay, you're okay" churches on the extreme left keep us from acknowledging our sin and brokenness. They treat sin as an illusion and fail to see how sin keeps us from being the people God desires. This theologically liberal approach may allow us to accept other people as they are, but it does not leave much room for spiritual growth or see any need for it. If we are unwilling to admit we are not okay, we cut ourselves off from the potential for change and transformation. God does not want us to pretend to be perfect when we are not. He wants us to acknowledge our need for grace and to recognize that we all have access to it through Christ Jesus. Redemption may be painful, but it is freeing. And in the end, the pain of redemption releases us from a deeper pain—the pain of our past. It destroys the bonds of guilt and shame. It offers us a future filled with faith, hope, and love. It may even offer us a future where we too can be content with "weakness, insults, hardships, persecutions, and calamities."

Action Step #6

At Salem Covenant Church, we call our small groups "growth groups." These groups meet monthly at the homes of designated church members. Small group facilitators are assigned to each group. This system allows the host to focus on hospitality and the discussion leader to focus on leading the conversation. Small groups can help your church members get to know one another better and learn from one another. Small groups function best when they invite people to tell their stories and to share about what is going on in their lives. Most people find it is easier to "be themselves" in small group settings. Small groups encourage people to be honest and open, which is a necessary step for building honest to God churches.

Education is an essential part of developing an honest to God approach. I encourage you to set up small groups to study the discussion questions in this book. Your pastors and leaders should also take advantage of every opportunity they have to speak about and teach the grace-based concepts in this book. These concepts can be taught from the pulpit; in Bible studies, adult Sunday school, confirmation, and new member classes; and through informal conversations with church members. If these concepts are to become a part of the culture of your congregation, church leaders must seek a variety of opportunities to share them and must model humble, accepting, and gracious approaches to doing ministry in general. The simple act of teaching the defining characteristics of an "I'm not okay, you're not okay" approach can have a tremendous impact on the life of your congregation.

Discussion Questions

1. When in your life do typically feel like using the phrase "Enough is enough"?
2. What are some of the things you hope God will do in your life apart from salvation?
3. What does the word *sufficient* mean?
4. If Jesus did not do anything else for you apart from what he did on the cross, is that sufficient for you?
5. What is the significance of the temple curtain being torn in two when Jesus breathed his last breath?
6. What challenges in your own life help you to understand how Brennan Manning became an alcoholic after he became a Christian?
7. Why do some people believe that an irreversible sinless future beckons after we accept Jesus into our lives?
8. Why is redemption at times a painful process?
9. In what ways can pain be a good thing for our lives?
10. Why did Peter feel hurt when Jesus asked him a third time if he loved him?
11. Have you ever felt like you were disappointing God or letting Jesus down because of something you said, did, or did not do? How did this impact your spiritual journey?
12. Why is it that certain things, which hurt our ego, are good for our soul?

Part Two

Honest to God Disciples

Seven

First Steps

A *few years ago, I heard a Hollywood news report on the* radio that said that Courtney Love, the lead singer for the punk band Hole, was released from a drug rehab facility and was seen going to church with one of her relatives. Courtney Love was the wife of the late Kurt Cobain, the lead singer of the grunge band Nirvana, who committed suicide at the peak of his career in the 1990s. She has since developed an infamous reputation as a promiscuous, drug abusing, troubled rock star. Love's painful struggles have been well documented in the tabloids. The morning host of this local radio show laughed at the Hollywood news report and responded by shouting, "Church?" followed by a chuckle.

The notion of Courtney Love going to church was utterly absurd from his perspective, but it should not shock Christians that church is one of the first places she sought out after going to rehab. This is an obvious first step if you understand the power and meaning of God's grace and the spiritual approach to recovery embraced by many drug and alcohol rehab programs. Often people in rehab feel God's grace powerfully. Therefore, going to church afterward makes absolute sense. Yet I wonder how much grace Courtney Love experienced at the church she visited. Were the people there able to see her need for grace and fulfill it? Or were they distracted by her fame, reputation, or appearance?

New Beginnings

In Alcoholics Anonymous the way people begin their spiritual journeys toward sobriety is by admitting that they have a problem. I believe the church can learn a thing or two in this regard from those involved with Alcoholics Anonymous. I am not an alcoholic, but I have helped a number of people discover sobriety through the work of Alcoholics Anonymous. I also regularly attend AA anniversary meetings with these friends who have been sober for more than a year. I have a deep level of admiration and appreciation for the way this program works. Also, one of my best friends has been a recovering alcoholic for more than twenty-five years, and I have learned a lot from him about the program and how it helps people. Theologian Dallas Willard writes in *Renovation of the Heart:*

> Historically, the A.A. program was closely aligned with the church and Christian traditions, and now it has much to give back to a church that has largely lost its grip on spiritual formation as a standard path of Christian life. Any successful plan for spiritual formation, whether for the individual or group will in fact be significantly similar to the Alcoholics Anonymous program.[1]

Throughout the remainder of this book, I will share more information about AA and its twelve steps, because there is much we and our congregations can learn from them. One need not be an alcoholic to take advantage of these twelve steps for spiritual growth, for the steps present pathways for all people to grow spiritually, and they are consistent with what Scripture and Christianity teach us about the process of redemption. They also provide a framework for the "I'm not okay, you're not okay" approach to develop more completely and to be utilized more effectively. These steps offer us insight into how we can reach out to broken people without falling into the trap of the "I'm okay, you're okay" approach.

Alcoholics Anonymous and all other twelve-step programs begin with the basic premise that the participants are not okay. There is a saying in AA that goes, "Once an alcoholic, always an alcoholic." This is why members are considered *recovering* alcoholics, not *recovered* ones. Martin Luther's understanding of Christians as being saints and sinners simultaneously carries the same idea. AA offers people the space and freedom to keep changing over time. Christians need to do the same for one another.

In *Healing the Shame That Binds You,* John Bradshaw, a counselor specializing in addictions and family systems, lists the twelve steps for healing what he calls toxic shame. These twelve steps are based on the model of Alcoholics Anonymous, and they have also been used by a number of other twelve-step support groups. The steps are always stated in the past tense. The first three steps encourage the healing process to begin. The first step states, "We admitted that we were powerless over (whatever the addiction) and that our lives had become unmanageable." If you are not addicted to anything in particular, you may want to say, "We admitted that we were powerless over *our shame* and that our lives had become unmanageable." The second step states, "We came to believe that a power greater than ourselves could restore us to sanity." For Christians, this greater power should be viewed as God's grace. It is God's grace that restores us to sanity. The third step states, "We made a decision to turn our will and our lives over to the care of God as we understand God."[2]

The first three steps in AA force persons to admit that they have a problem. They also ask recovering alcoholics to surrender to God and to learn how to depend on God's grace rather than on their own strength for sobriety. What I see in AA that I do not see enough of in the church is an open and honest search for change within our personal lives. AA clearly has an "I'm not okay, you're not okay" approach to helping alcoholics. AA's primary purpose is to help recovering alcoholics to stay sober and to help other alcoholics achieve sobriety.

The reason John Bradshaw calls his plan "the twelve steps for healing toxic shame" is because shame lies at the root of all compulsive and addictive behavior. Shame is a direct consequence of our sin and our being sinned against. It is one of the primary reasons we need God and each other. It also exists as one of the major distractions in our Christian discipleship. Shame keeps us from embracing an "I'm not okay, you're not okay" approach, because it makes us feel as if we need to hide from one another and from God. Our fear of being exposed keeps us from being our true selves, and it keeps us from living out our faith in an authentic way.

Saying that we have something to learn from AA is not to say that AA has everything in life figured out or that people in AA do not need the church. People in AA need the church and Jesus in addition to their experiences in the program. Alcoholics Anonymous helps alcoholics deal with their alcoholism. However, alcoholism is merely a symptom of the more profound problems of sin, shame, and pain that plague a person's life. The church can help people in the AA program address these broader issues in a deeper way.

Space for Grace

Courtney Love's story reveals that everyone needs to start his or her spiritual journey in the church somewhere. Her story also reveals how wrong it is for churches to expect people to be finished straightening out their lives before they get started serving in their communities and ministries. New people coming into our churches are often in a state of crisis. They need to experience God's grace, and they need to be introduced to it in a gentle way, because the human soul is often filled with fear and can easily be frightened.

I love the account in Luke 7:36–50 about a sinner who came to see Jesus while he was eating in the house of a Pharisee. A woman from the city heard Jesus was there and brought an alabaster jar of ointment. The text says that she "stood behind him at his feet, weeping, and began to bathe his feet with her tears and to dry them with her hair. Then she continued kissing his feet and anointing them with the ointment." The Pharisee was taken aback by her presence and actions, as well as surprised that Jesus let her touch him in this way. The Pharisee said to himself, "If this man were a prophet, he would have known who and what kind of woman this is who is touching him—that she is a sinner."

Jesus then shared a parable with the Pharisee and asked this question: "A certain creditor had two debtors; one owed five hundred denarii, and the other fifty. When they could not pay, he canceled the debts for both of them. Now which of them will love him more?" Simon the Pharisee responded, "I suppose the one for whom he canceled the greater debt." And Jesus said to him, "You have judged rightly."

Jesus's point was not that God wants us to sin more so that we have more debt to forgive. Rather, Jesus told this story so the Pharisee would understand why Jesus was allowing a sinful woman to touch his feet. He wanted the Pharisee to understand how important it is to allow space for grace to work in the hearts and lives of sinners. And by extension, he was teaching us to create this kind of space for grace to work in the church today. People need time to change, and it is up to us to give it to them.

Courtney Love's fame is not the reason this church should have looked beyond her reputation as a troubled individual. They should have looked beyond her troubles because she is a human being and a child of God. They should have looked beneath her reputation into her soul. They should have allowed her to be herself and to experience God's grace on a deeper level. She should have been given permission to start a new phase in her life that would be unencumbered by her reputation or her fame.

After Jesus shared the parable about the creditor and the two debtors with Simon, he turned to the woman who had anointed his feet, and said to the Pharisee:

> Do you see this woman? I entered your house; you gave me no water for my feet, but she has bathed my feet with her tears and dried them with her hair. You gave me no kiss, but from the time I came in she has not stopped kissing my feet. You did not anoint my head with oil, but she has anointed my feet with ointment. Therefore, I tell you, her sins, which were many, have been forgiven; hence she has shown great love. But the one to whom little is forgiven, loves little.

Through his parable and teaching of this Pharisee, Jesus points to a spiritual advantage that sinful people have over those who have lived more righteous lives. He reveals that those who have lived more righteously can benefit by welcoming sinners into their churches in the same way Jesus welcomed them into his life. Churches that have an open-door policy for known sinners will have more life in their ministries because of the amount of forgiven debt in their midst. Everyone will share in the excitement and enthusiasm generated by God's grace.

Honesty

God wants us to be honest with him, one another, and ourselves as we move through the process of redemption. When we become Christians, we begin a lifelong journey of growth and learning, but we all have to take the first few steps. And beginning the process may be the most challenging aspect of it. In Philippians 2:1–2, the apostle Paul writes, "If then there is any encouragement in Christ, any consolation from love, any sharing in the Spirit, any compassion and sympathy, make my joy complete: be of the same mind, having the same love, being in full accord, and of one mind." Note that this passage does not say, "If you are *completely* encouraged by Christ, *absolutely* consoled by love, *fully* sharing in the Spirit, and *totally* compassionate and sympathetic. . . ." Rather, it says, "If there is *any* encouragement . . . *any* consolation . . . *any* sharing . . . *any* compassion and sympathy. . . ." Even if we have a little glimpse of the truth or an inkling of understanding or an element of concern for others, we are called to "get on board." We should not wait until all of our theological questions are answered and all of our doubts are done away with before we begin our journey with Christ.

The good news about God's grace is that Jesus meets us in the midst of our mess. Where there is pain, Jesus is there. Where there is brokenness, Jesus is there. Where there is sin, Jesus is there. In turn we hope there is enough encouragement in Christ, enough consolation from love, enough sharing in the Spirit, and enough compassion and sympathy within all of our experiences to draw us into this process of redemption and into the life-changing power of God's almighty grace.

To become an honest to God disciple, we must acknowledge our need for God's grace and God's people. We all have sin, shame, and pain in our lives and experience loneliness, depression, and confusion at times. In the church, however, we must be willing to admit to our brokenness before we can begin this process of redemption. Admitting our need for grace is a huge first step. Acknowledging our human weakness and vulnerability allows us to be more open to God and one another in the church.

Recognizing our need for God's grace allows us to rely on his grace more completely. Surrendering to God and learning how to rely on his grace more than our strength are not only the keys to becoming sober; they are also the keys to becoming disciples. It should not surprise us that there are parallels between the spiritual journeys of recovery and discipleship, for both have the same intention, which is to transform lives and offer new beginnings. This kind of honest to God approach will have a huge impact on our lives because it will allow God's grace to work in the way it is supposed to, one person at a time and one step at a time.

Discipleship Step #1

In our quest to become honest to God disciples, we must do more than acknowledge our need for grace. We must also actively seek to receive God's grace by acknowledging our sinfulness and brokenness through prayer. We must surrender our lives to God on our knees. We must step back from all the good things we strive to accomplish in our lives and allow something good to happen to us. We must openly receive God's grace into our hearts, for God wants grace to saturate our lives. As followers of Jesus, we need to believe not only in the existence of God, but in the effectiveness of his grace as well.

Journaling is one spiritual discipline that can help us become more fully aware of the depth of our need for grace. Through journaling we can thoughtfully consider how we are doing on a spiritual level. Journaling opens a window through which we can examine our relationships with God and become more aware of our spiritual needs. Journaling also allows us to recognize and reflect on our experiences with God's grace in the past. Recalling moments when we have encountered God's grace can keep us from taking grace for granted.

Writing down these stories about grace not only makes us more aware of how God has helped us in the past, but it also helps us to be clearer about the path God has established for our future. Go out and purchase a journal. Then begin writing about your spiritual life. Write about your spiritual needs and challenges. Also write down as many stories as you can about how God's grace has impacted your life. Journaling is a great way to identify your spiritual needs and to become more aware of the spiritual resources you have to rely on.

Discussion Questions

1. Why do you think the local radio announcer laughed when he heard that Courtney Love went to church? Was it her reputation or the church's reputation that he was laughing at?
2. Why do you think Courtney Love went to church?
3. What kind of church would keep a person like Courtney Love coming back?
4. What keeps people from being honest about their personal struggles with each other in the church?
5. What is vulnerability, and why is it important to spirituality?
6. How are the first steps in Alcoholics Anonymous similar to the first steps in becoming a disciple?
7. What do you know about the spiritual side of Alcoholics Anonymous? What do you think the church can learn from AA about spiritual formation?
8. How can being honest about your personal struggles help you to grow spiritually?
9. How could your church do a better job of encouraging people to be more honest about where they are at in life as they become Christians and try to build Christian lives?
10. Why is the first step one of the most difficult ones to take in the process of redemption? Do you find the use of the word "any" in Philippians 2:1–3 helpful in this regard?
11. How has your experience of God's grace changed your life or your perspective on life?
12. Why do some people resist receiving God's grace?

Eight

~~~~~

Sin and Shame

I *once heard a friend of mine speak to a large group of sixth* and seventh graders at Pilgrim Pines, a Christian camp in New Hampshire. She spoke with these young people about how much God loves them and others. While speaking, she took out a bag of Skittles candy and asked if any of them wanted it. The room erupted with enthusiasm. Everyone wanted the candy. Then she threw the bag on the floor and stomped on it. She asked them again, and still almost everyone in the room wanted the candy. Then she opened the bag and spat in it, allowing a few others to make contributions as well. After this, no one wanted the candy, except one kid who wanted to be the center of attention.

The speaker then took out a twenty dollar bill and asked the students if they wanted it. The place again erupted with enthusiasm. She then stomped on and soiled the twenty-dollar bill in the same way she did the candy, but this time everyone still wanted the money. They understood that no matter what anyone did to it, the money would not lose its value. She then urged the students to recognize that no matter what happens to them, they do not lose their value. Because we all are created in the image of God, we never lose our value, no matter how much we get kicked around or spat upon in our lives.

Guilt

Shame often prevents us from understanding our value as human beings. Genesis 2:25 tells us that at the time of creation "the man and his wife were both naked, and were not ashamed." Then, after they ate of the forbidden fruit in Genesis 3:7, we read, "Then the eyes of both were opened, and they knew that they were naked; and they sewed fig leaves together and made loincloths for themselves." This verse gives us a vivid picture of shame, and this story describes the relationship between sin and shame. Adam and Eve ate the forbidden fruit and were ashamed, and they hid themselves from God and from each other.

This passage in Genesis does not say anything about guilt. Yet many in the church have been led to believe that it is about guilt and, therefore, that it is their duty to rescue people from their guilty consciences. Worse yet, some people feel it is their responsibility to make others feel guilty so they will seek God's grace. I know some preachers who feel good about making people feel bad on Sunday mornings. These pastors and church leaders are convinced that people need to feel more guilt before they will be prepared to admit to the sin in their lives and seek forgiveness.

The problem resulting from this way of thinking is that people who enter into those churches are given the impression that they do not feel bad enough about themselves, which is a shock, because most people feel plenty bad about themselves already. Adding to people's shame by focusing on their need for more guilt makes the problem worse. We often confuse shame with guilt. Shame and guilt are related, but they are not one in the same. Guilt feeds into shame, but shame is a much deeper emotional reality. Guilt is the bad feeling we get when we do something wrong. Shame is the sense we have about ourselves that there is something wrong with us.

Feeling guilty is not a bad thing. We should feel guilty when we do something wrong. Imagine a society in which people did not feel any guilt. Guilt deserves credit, not criticism, for it is an emotion that can keep us from doing the wrong thing. Moreover, it enables us to repent and apologize when we do something wrong. If we believe there is a difference between right and wrong, we are going to feel bad when we say or do wrong things and fail to do the right things.

Shame is deeper than guilt, and it is our distorted levels of shame that keep us from being our true selves. Too much shame keeps us from experiencing joy and being grateful for the things we should be grateful for in our lives. John Bradshaw refers to shame as the "core demon" that has plagued his life. He said that "naming shame" changed everything for him.[1]

Shame, the primary emotional consequence of sin, is something we don't often talk about even though it affects us all. Shame is mysterious. It is related to our deepest and most private emotions and emotional problems. The reality of shame is often very painful. Shame cannot be removed entirely from our lives, but we can learn to keep it in perspective and to minimize its negative impact on us. This is often difficult because shame impacts us on a variety of levels.

Nakedness, the image used in Genesis 2 and 3, is a great image for helping us to understand our shame. Early in my marriage, and not long after I started preaching, my wife enjoyed privately saying the phrase, "I've seen you naked." She particularly liked to say this on Sunday afternoons when we got home from our worship services. She was saying that nothing in my life was hidden from her. She was getting used to the fact that her husband was now the pastor of the church in which she worshiped. What I think she meant was that she knows me on a deeper level than the other people in my church. She was casting a light on the fact that her relationship with me was unique and more intimate. She also did not want me to begin thinking about myself more highly than I should.

When we are naked or imagine ourselves to be naked in front of others, we feel vulnerable. We are afraid of what others will think about all of our imperfections and inadequacies. We worry about how we look. We worry about our size and our shape. We worry about all the things that concern God the least. And we, therefore, hide from each other and God. Many of us have had dreams about finding ourselves naked in situations where we would otherwise be wearing clothes. I have never been much for interpreting dreams, but it seems to me that these dreams reveal our experience with shame and how it affects our lives. Shame leads us to feel naked even while we have all of our clothes on. Genesis 3:8–11 says:

> They heard the sound of the LORD God walking in the garden at the time of the evening breeze, and the man and his wife hid themselves from the presence of the LORD God among the trees of the garden. But the LORD God called to the man, and said to him, "Where are you?" He said, "I heard the sound of you in the garden, and I was afraid, because I was naked; and I hid myself." He said, "Who told you that you were naked? Have you eaten from the tree of which I commanded you not to eat?"

Shame can so take over our lives that we lose perspective on who we are. This spiritual consequence of sin can become so amplified that we lose sight of our identity as God's children. Deep levels of shame can be isolating, alienating, and even debilitating. It is one thing to have a sense that there is something wrong with you; it is something else altogether to have the sense that there is something more wrong with you than everyone else around you. Yet this is how our shame often makes us feel.

Shame

Shame exists in our lives, like it or not. Shame is the primary emotional consequence of sin. Some people distinguish between types of shame. John Bradshaw distinguishes between "nourishing shame" and "toxic shame."[2] Lewis Smedes differentiated between "healthy shame" and "unhealthy shame."[3] I believe there are different levels of shame, not necessarily different types. Some people experience too much shame, whereas others don't experience enough. Appropriate levels of shame keep us in touch with our humanity. Lewis Smedes said, "Pornographers are shameless. This does not mean that—like Adam and Eve—they are unashamed; it means that they have lost their power to feel shame. To that extent they have lost their souls."[4] Another way to say this is to say that they have lost their human dignity. People without dignity fail to experience shame. They experience an emotional disconnection from their lives. An appropriate level of shame within our lives is a good thing. The low levels of shame most of us experience naturally within our lives remind us that we are sinners and that we need God and each other.

After eating the forbidden fruit from the tree of the knowledge of good and evil, Adam and Eve were ashamed of their nakedness and hid from each other and from God, but God eventually gave them something to cover themselves with. Genesis 3:21 says, "The LORD God made garments of skins for the man and for his wife, and clothed them." Allowing ourselves to be covered up to a certain point is a normal response to the realities of sin and shame in our lives, but because of the amount of shame that has typically come into many of our lives, we have taken the loin cloths that were initially provided by God and turned them into full-blown costumes that not only cover up our nakedness, but also our true identity.

At North Park University, chapel services were not mandatory for the staff or students, but as staff, I felt obligated to attend as much as possible. The chaplain appreciated our attendance, and I felt she expected us to be there to support the chapel program. One day I was planning on attending chapel, but a student came to me in a state of crisis. She was in tears and needed to talk immediately. I did the right thing. I skipped chapel and met with this student. However, by the time the chapel service ended, I was walking through the center of campus and saw the chaplain coming toward me. I did not feel guilty, because I had done the right thing, but I did feel ashamed. I felt ashamed because I was afraid that the chaplain probably thought I had done something wrong and possibly even that there was something wrong with me.

This fear was most likely unfounded. The chaplain probably did not think twice about my missing chapel that day. It was my shame and insecurity that created the problem. The reason shame is universal is because sin is universal. The reason we all have a sense that there is something wrong with us is because *there is* something wrong with us. Romans 3:23–24 says, "Since all have sinned and fall short of the glory of God; they are now justified by his grace as a gift, through the redemption that is in Christ Jesus." I have yet to meet a person who is unable to say that they have sinned and fallen short of God's glory.

In twelve-step support groups, the fourth step states, "We made a searching and fearless moral inventory of ourselves." The fifth step states, "We admitted to God, to ourselves, and to another human being the exact nature of our wrongs." The sixth step continues, "We were entirely ready to have God remove all these defects of character." These are followed by the seventh step, which says, "We humbly asked God to remove our shortcomings."[5] Not many Christian churches today are encouraging this kind of self-examination in the lives of their members. One of the primary reasons for this is that we do not trust God enough. We have not really accepted God's acceptance of us, so we do not feel safe doing this type of moral inventory in most church environments.

Jesus said in Luke 12:1–3, "Beware of the yeast of the Pharisees, that is, their hypocrisy. Nothing is covered up that will not be uncovered, and nothing secret that will not become known. Therefore whatever you have said in the dark will be heard in the light, and whatever you have whispered behind closed doors will be proclaimed from the housetops." Churches need to move beyond their fear of moral self-examination. We need to place more trust in God's grace. We need to realize that we cannot hide from God even though this may be one of our deepest desires as sinful human beings.

Grace is an antithesis to shame. This is why the church's failure to distinguish between shame and guilt has left it ill equipped to interact appropriately with people and their sin. Instead of offering God's grace to help people deal with their shame, we often send messages that feed their shame. We have developed guilt-inducing theologies that shame instead of shame-reducing theologies that build up people. Because of this gross misunderstanding, churches are missing many opportunities to reveal God's grace to people and to help them enter into life-changing relationships with Jesus Christ.

The church's preoccupation with the feeling of guilt has probably been one of the most damaging realities in the church's history, yet much of the church is completely unaware of it. Most people do not see themselves as wicked, evil, or wretched, because they are not. Thus, the more that church leaders push people to feel this way, the more these people begin to think there is something more amiss with the church leaders than there is with themselves. Sadly, many preachers experience a great deal of shame themselves. This confuses them personally and interferes with their preaching of the good news.

Shame-based preaching that focuses on making people feel guilty turns people away from the church rather than drawing them into it. This kind of preaching keeps people from experiencing God's grace because of its lack of grace. Failing to understand the implications of shame limits the church's effectiveness and alienates people who want and need to hear the gospel. The church needs good news preachers of grace, not bad news proclaimers of shame. We need to look for healing tears as we preach, not squirming bodies. Shame and the church's failure to understand it have left many pastors feeling abandoned by the larger church.

There is a good reason why the first chapter and a half of Genesis appears before the second chapter and a half. The first chapter and a half focus on the goodness of creation and on the fact that we as human beings were created good in God's image. It says, "In the image of God he created them; male and female he created them" (Gen. 1:27). God would not have sent Jesus into the world if he did not love us. John 3:16 begins, "God so loved the world that he gave his only Son." We may not be entitled to God's grace, but this does not mean that we are completely unworthy of it. We do not earn God's grace, but this does not mean that we are rotten, wicked, and worthless. We are God's children, created uniquely in his image. God loves us because he made us and because we are his children. We belong to him. His grace is a gift of love, and we are the objects of that love.

Discipleship Step #2

In our quest to become honest to God disciples, we must become more honest with ourselves and God. In the twelve steps of Alcoholics Anonymous, people make a searching and fearless moral inventory of their lives. Even though this type of personal inquiry is not something churches typically encourage Christians to do, it would be helpful. Most Christians would benefit by getting their eyes off the sins of others and onto their own sinfulness. A searching and fearless moral inventory will help us understand that we are sinners and in need of God's grace on a deeper level. It will help us to repent of our sins and be humble with regard to the sinfulness of others. It will also help to guard us against self-righteousness and judgmentalism.

In a church setting, people ought to be encouraged to set aside time to make a list of all the people they have hurt in their lifetime. Then they should be encouraged to find a person they trust, such as a pastor, a prayer partner, a spiritual director, or a counselor, with whom they can share this information. Making amends with the people you have hurt can be done effectively only after you have personally acknowledged your offenses. Asking for God's forgiveness and healing are also an essential part of this redeeming process. This is a step-by-step process. You should not move on to the other steps until the first few have been taken. In AA people are encouraged to make sure they have the first three steps taken care of before they move on to the fourth step. This searching and fearless moral inventory is seen as a very significant action. Christians should view it in the same way.

Discussion Questions

1. What is sin?
2. Why do some preachers feel good about making people feel bad on Sunday mornings?
3. What is the difference between shame and guilt?
4. Which is the deeper emotional consequence of sin—guilt or shame?
5. How does the image of nakedness help us to understand the meaning of shame?
6. In what ways can shame be nourishing and helpul?
7. How does it feel to acknowledge that you have sinned and fallen short of God's glory in your life?
8. Why is feeling guilty about the bad things you do a good thing?
9. In what ways can feeling like there is something more wrong with us than everyone else around us be debilitating?
10. In what ways are we both unworthy and worthy of God's grace at the same time?
11. If we do not earn grace, why does God want us to experience it?

Nine

~~~~~~

Secrets and Lies

S *everal years ago a woman came to our church because her* church would not baptize her child. She wanted me to baptize the child, even though she was not married to the child's father, with whom she was living. Her eldest child had been regularly attending our Sunday school program, but the mother had only started to attend worship after her second child was born. When she asked me if I would baptize her son, I was determined to be as gracious as I could be. My desire was to offer this sacrament of grace without any hesitation. I said yes almost immediately. Once I made my willingness to perform the baptism clear, we talked about why she had not married the child's father. I listened as she shared her opinions and experiences. She spoke boldly about not believing in the institution of marriage because of all its failures. What is most interesting is that a few Sundays after I baptized her child, she was leaving worship and showed me a diamond ring on her finger. I said, "You're engaged." She said, "No, I got married."

Secrets

Churches often use the sacraments of grace as leverage to manip- ulate people's behavior. Many clergy who feel powerless in their leadership positions seek more authority by using and abusing the sacraments. It is heartbreaking that the people manipulated by this misuse of clerical power often are those most in need of God's mercy. Grace offers no guarantees, but many times it leads to more significant and long-lasting change in the lives of those to whom we minister. When people reach for grace and find judgment, they typically turn away from the church and fail to make it a part of their lives. This kind of judgment also creates an environment in which people are afraid to be themselves when they come to church. It forces them to be dishonest with themselves, each other, and God.

I remember that when living in Chicago, I observed a neighborhood development agency that invested a significant amount of time and money offering grants to store owners for facade improvements. The store owners were typically most concerned about investing their money in their inventory, but the neighborhood development agency wanted the stores to improve their appearance to make the neighborhood more inviting. This neighborhood development agency not only wanted to help existing stores, but also to attract new store owners who would feel good about having businesses in an attractive neighborhood.

Facades are important, but they only take you so far. An improved facade might get people to enter a store for the first time, but it will never lead people to become regular customers. In recent years the media has carried stories about several sleazy furniture stores that have gotten into trouble for selling used mattresses with new ticking on them. On the outside the mattresses looked new, but on the inside they were disgusting, bug-infested, dirt-ridden mattresses. Most of the facades we have created in our lives are not covering up to this extent, but they can feel like it. We often feel like used mattresses covered with new ticking, and we need to figure out some way to improve our inner lives so the insides and the outsides match more closely. Paying attention to our souls, not just our egos, allows us to develop our inner lives more fully. I once heard someone at an

AA meeting say, "We should not compare our insides to other people's outsides."

Facades provide us with important defense mechanisms. They help us to cope with the details and stresses of daily life. Nevertheless, we all know there is a difference between telling a lie and living one. Defense mechanisms that cover up our shame become problematic when we end up trusting no one with our personal information. If we feel that we need to hide all the time, shame begins to consume our lives and rob us of our dignity. When this occurs, shame and anxiety rise to dangerously high levels, and the facade we have built begins to crumble and our lives spin out of control. We then hurt not only ourselves but often others, such as family members and coworkers.

Lies

There is nothing wrong with practicing discretion, but keeping painful secrets buried within our souls will inevitably reap destruction because of the large amount of deception necessary to keep them from being exposed. Family secrets often lead us down the path of self-deception. They are usually kept with the intention of "protecting" one another. They happen any time one family member tells someone something and then says, "But don't tell your mother (or whoever else is being protected from this secret information)." Big family secrets like abortions, incarcerations, mental illness, adoptions, divorces, addictions, or suicides often lead to a wide variety of smaller secrets that divide families and keep them from functioning properly. Edwin Friedman, a rabbi and family therapist specializing in family systems and congregational life, writes, "Family secrets act as the plaque in the arteries of communication; they cause stoppage in the general flow and not just at the point of their existence."[1]

Jesus's encounter with the woman at the well in John 4 reveals how secrets impact our lives. Because she was a Samaritan and a female, the woman was surprised that Jesus would speak to her. And because she had lived a sinful life, she felt certain he would not be talking to her if he knew much, if anything, about her. In the middle of Jesus's conversation with this woman, he revealed that he knew everything about her background. He said, "Go, call your husband, and come back." The woman replied, "I have no husband." Jesus, in turn, responded, "You are right in saying, 'I have no husband'; for you have had five husbands, and the one you now have is not your husband" (vv. 16–18).

When this woman initially approached the well, she expected that Jesus would treat her as if she were invisible, but he did not. He asked her for a drink—from her cup no less. Jesus did not just talk to her. He spoke with her about some rather deep theological and personal issues. Jesus demonstrated a type of respect she did not expect—especially after he revealed that he knew everything there was to know about her life. He uncovered her shame, yet he stayed. The testimony that she shared later with the Samaritans in the city was "Come and see a man who told me everything I have ever done!" (v. 29). Jesus set her free from the prison that her life had become.

When stores sell products with many layers underneath the visible exterior, such as a pair of shoes, a mattress, or a couch, I appreciate when the company cuts a sample of the product in half so I can see what lies underneath. I feel better if the people selling the product feel comfortable showing customers what is on the inside. It shows that they are confident in their product and materials. Transparency and authenticity are essential in our lives and in our intimate relationships. Divulging every-thing about ourselves to everyone we meet is not necessary. But we must have relationships with some people whom we trust and with whom we can share our deepest feelings and secrets. Vulnerability leads us toward God's grace and more intimate relationships with one another. This is why churches must create emotional environments that allow people to be themselves and to face the issues in their lives that exist beneath the surface.

Soul and Ego

The distinction between soul and ego is an important one with regard to the layers in our lives that exist below the surface. The ego is the part of us fed by things like success, awards, good grades, compliments, trophies, job promotions, and pay raises. Conversely, the soul is the part of us fed by intimacy, long walks, friendships, Bible study, family, outreach, worship, fellowship, service, and prayer. The soul is fed by experiences that remind us we are human, that we are in real relationships with other human beings, and that we are in a real relationship with God. When the ego is well fed, we are often able to hide our true selves behind well-constructed facades. The problem is that a malnourished soul can exist beneath a well-nourished ego, and if the ego falls apart, the person is left helpless and hopeless.

The things the ego desires are not the same as the things the soul needs. More often than not we pay too much attention to the ego and not enough to the soul. The problem is not that we have an ego. The problem is that we live in a society that pays so much attention to the ego that we often end up neglecting the soul. Typically it takes a life crisis to get us to pay more attention to our souls.

Keith Miller, author of the best-selling book *Taste of New Wine*, wrote a book called *The Secret Life of the Soul* after he went through an ego crash. In it he suggests that going to therapy or counseling after an ego crash to try to rebuild the ego is sort of like trying to "redecorate a burning house."[2] He suggests that a person has to pay attention to rebuilding the soul before the ego will ever be able to breathe again. He describes his ego crash this way: "My marriage of twenty-seven years was over . . . finished! My vocational life as a Christian writer and speaker was about to shrivel and atrophy. Yet something else had ended, something even deeper and more frightening: Was it my life? No, I was still alive, although I was numb. Still it felt as if the person I'd always imagined myself to be was dying."[3] When our egos are strong, we often hide behind them and our souls do not develop. We feel safe when other people think our lives are successful. But when our egos are allowed to develop and our souls are not, our lives fall dangerously out of balance. The ego-driven part of our lives starts to feel fake. We begin to feel fake, and our souls are left untended and malnourished.

This is why Jesus, in the story of Jesus dining in the home of Mary and Martha, defends Mary and says she chose the better part. Luke 10:38 says, "Martha welcomed Jesus into her home." Then verses 39–42 say:

> [Martha] had a sister named Mary, who sat at the Lord's feet and listened to what he was saying. But Martha was distracted by her many tasks; so she came to him and asked, "Lord, do you not care that my sister has left me to do all the work by myself? Tell her then to help me." But the Lord answered her, "Martha, Martha, you are worried and distracted by many things; there is need of only one thing. Mary has chosen the better part, which will not be taken away from her."

Some women do not like this passage because women often are asked whether they are a "Mary" or a "Martha." The truth is, every woman has a little bit of both in herself. Jesus did not like Mary better than Martha. He loved them both. Jesus defended Mary because the world always defends Martha. Men tend to ignore this passage about Mary and Martha altogether because it is obviously about two women. But since when are women the only people who have to be concerned about finding a balance between the activity in their lives and quiet time with God? Since when are women the only people distracted by their many tasks?

Sometimes I find it helpful to change the names and story line in this passage to help men better identify with it. I change the names from Mary and Martha to Max and Marvin. Marvin invites Jesus on a fishing trip with him and his brother, Max. Marvin prepares for the trip by getting the nets and boat ready while Max sits at Jesus's feet soaking up everything he has to say. Marvin gets angry because Max is not doing his part. Jesus tells Marvin to relax because Max has chosen the better part, and he says this will not be taken from him. The truth is, there is a "Max" and "Marvin" or a "Mary" and "Martha" in all of us. We simply need to learn how to keep both in perspective. We each need to find a balance between the Max and Marvin or the Mary and Martha within us.

The key to developing spiritual maturity is to pay sufficient attention to the soul in a society that predominantly focuses on the ego. In an ideal situation, the ego and the soul would both be strong and well nourished, but we do not always have control over the things our egos experience. To a certain extent, we need our egos. That is part of what it means to be human. But we should never pay so much attention to our egos that we forget about our souls. More often than not, our ego-based society does not pay enough attention to the soul until the ego crashes or falls apart. Our lives can become overwhelmed and seem unmanageable when this happens.

Discipleship Step #3

In our quest to become honest to God disciples, we need to distinguish between the soul and the ego. We can do this best by writing down a list of things that feed our egos and a list of things that feed our souls. Once we have clarified the difference between these two parts of ourselves, we can begin to evaluate how much time and energy we are putting into feeding each of them. We must learn to create balance in our lives. We cannot get rid of our egos altogether, but we can learn to pay more attention to our souls. People with malnourished souls often experience ego crashes and are left unable to cope with their disappointments and challenges. Honest to God disciples need well-nourished souls. We should all strive to pray, study Scripture, walk, journal, fast, read, and serve others more than we currently do. We also need to discover people in our lives who naturally feed our souls and spend more time with them. Likewise, we need to discover the places that feed our souls and spend more time there.

To make sure you are paying enough attention to your soul, make a list of the things you do on a daily, weekly, monthly, and annual basis to feed your soul. Next, write down one way you could improve or enhance each area to provide more nourishment for your soul. Keeping these plans on your calendar is an important part of being an honest to God disciple. Knowing what feeds your soul is one thing; acting on it is something else altogether. Discipleship is a commitment and requires spiritual discipline. Spiritual disciplines help us to make room for God in our lives. They remind us to pray regularly and stay in touch with God. This is one way we acknowledge God's greatness and the fact that God is bigger than we are.

Discussion Questions

1. Why do we keep secrets?
2. How can secrets interfere with communication in families?
3. What is the difference between telling a lie and living one?
4. What are facades?
5. Why do we develop facades for our lives?
6. What happens to people who feel as if they have to hide from everyone all of the time?
7. What feeds your ego?
8. What feeds your soul?
9. What happens when a person pays too much attention to the ego and not enough attention to the soul?
10. What happens when people start paying more attention to their souls than their egos?

Ten

Sin and Pain

One Sunday morning, a member of our church came into my office to tell me about something that had happened to her over the weekend. She explained that she was attending a high school baseball game and was hit in the face by a line drive baseball. Her nose was fractured, her eye was badly bruised, and one side of her face was swollen. Even so, she said she was grateful that nothing worse had happened. She understood that if the ball had hit an inch to one side or the other, she could have been injured worse or even killed.

She came to me concerned because she kept having flashbacks about the event and was afraid there was something permanently wrong with her. She was worried that her flashbacks would never go away, because she had tried to make them stop and they did not. She had experienced a real trauma, and it is normal to relive an event like this mentally for a time. I told her that someone had once advised me not to resist such flashbacks, saying they were part of the healing process. Trying to repress them would only disrupt or slow down the healing process. I assured her it would simply take time for her to heal physically and emotionally from her experience.

Trauma

Most of the trauma we go through in life is far more tragic or personal in nature than the above example. I talk with many people whose experiences I cannot share because of the personal nature of their stories. Physical, sexual, emotional, and even spiritual abuse have in some way been a part of many of our lives. And we all have experienced a variety of loss, rejection, and neglect. We can heal from these particular incidences, but often they become a part of our collective memories and contribute to the distorted levels of shame and pain that exist in our lives. When shame and pain interact with each other, the mix can be volatile and can keep us from developing a proper emotional and spiritual balance in our lives.

One of the problems that has arisen from our preoccupation with guilt in modern Christianity is that we pay far too much attention to how sinning against others impacts us but not nearly enough time to how the sins others commit against us impact us. To put it boldly, we pay too much attention to the violators and not enough attention to those who have been violated. Sin is a double-edged sword. On the one hand, we feel bad when we do things we know we should not. On the other hand, we feel bad when other people do things to us that we know they should not. While this seems rather obvious, we Christians have placed too much focus on our sinful side and forgotten how God's grace also relates to our broken side.

The church has traditionally thought about grace as a cure for guilt when, in reality, it is the salve we apply to the deepest wounds of our souls. In this sense, the church has failed to grasp the magnitude of God's grace. Many think about the gospel only in terms of people sinning, feeling guilty, being forgiven, and then experiencing freedom from guilt. Neither people's lives nor God's grace are this linear or narrow in focus. This overly simplistic understanding of God's grace is the one most often presented by Christians and the Christian church; yet this linear or narrow understanding of God's grace fails to shed light on the dynamic and multidimensional nature of grace. We need a new understanding of all that God's grace can do for us. Changing the way we look at sin, shame, and pain can help us to serve people more effectively and to offer grace more enthusiastically.

In the church we often talk about what God's grace can do for people who experience guilt, but we don't talk much about what God's grace can do for those who experience pain. Pain is a deep part of many of our lives. Pain feeds our shame just as shame feeds our pain. Pain and shame are the two primary realities that plague our souls. Many people enter our churches feeling abused and beaten down by life. They need to know that there is nothing in our lives that God is not aware of and is not willing to face with us. God does not, however, force himself on us. God's grace is available, but we must make room for it to work.

Pain

Pain is not always a bad thing. In fact, it can have a redemptive impact on our lives. Some pain strengthens us. As a parent, I often feel a very strong protective instinct toward my children. Part of me never wants my daughters to experience pain, yet I know that pain is a part of life and that learning early to deal with it will enable them to better cope with the challenges they will encounter as adults. In her book *After the Darkest Hour,* Dr. Kathleen A. Brehony discusses how children need to experience pain as a means of developing resilience. "Numerous research studies have shown that adversity and trials in childhood that don't overwhelm can strengthen a child's self-confidence and lay down the bedrock for future resiliency in life's difficult times."[1]

Resiliency is the ability to cope with the pain and struggles we face in life. Young people who do not experience enough pain and struggle during childhood are typically not very

resilient. Brehony points out that there are limits, however, to
how productive human pain can be for children. She writes,
"Many of the world's children suffer hardships that far outweigh
their abilities to cope. Starvation, violence, poverty, abuse, or
devastating illness greatly exceeds what might be thought of as
'optimal.'"[2] When children are abused, the sinful adults who
abuse them cross over boundaries that violate this line that exists between enough pain and too much pain. Abusive behavior
keeps young people from developing emotionally at a normal
pace with their peers. When abuse occurs, souls are crushed, and
the spiritual curiosity children normally experience is smothered.
Their dignity is stolen.

No child or adult should have to experience an overabun-
dance of pain and humiliation. But sadly, people do. Abuse
often imprisons people in shame. Abuse leaves individuals with
a strong sense that there is something more wrong with them
than with those around them. This is the point at which shame
becomes toxic. Abuse makes people feel unworthy to receive
anything good, including love. There is a very clear difference
between sin and abuse. All abuse is sin, but not all sin is abuse.
Abuse is when people take advantage of power or positions and
injure or manipulate others to satisfy something sick within
themselves.

The strange thing is that abusive behavior is often passed
down from one generation to another. People who are abused
sometimes end up becoming abusers themselves. On the surface,
this reality does not make any sense. Why would people fall into
the same hurtful patterns that created so much pain in their
own lives? Why would they want to follow in the footsteps of
those who ruined their lives and robbed them of their dignity?
Consciously, no one wants to do that. It does not make sense,
because abuse does not make sense.

Abusive behavior is often compulsive and grows out of the
sickness and pain that come from being abused in the first place.
It grows out of a cycle of shame and pain that consumes those

caught up in it. The shame that consumes abused people is the same shame that leads them to become abusers themselves. This dynamic reveals how destructive and dark the mix of shame and pain can be and how important it is that we develop a better grip on it.

Addiction

Shame and pain can also merge in our lives in the area of compulsive or addictive behaviors. When people come to me to talk about behavioral issues, they rarely focus on their guilt. Typically they come because they feel that particular aspects of their lives are out of control. Distorted levels of shame are what lead people into compulsive and addictive behaviors. John Bradshaw's working definition of this type of behavior is "a pathological relationship to any mood-altering experience that has life-damaging consequences." He illustrates this by writing, "I used to drink to solve the problems caused by drinking."[3] This certainly relates to alcohol, but it can also relate to addictions such as gambling, drugs, food, work, sex, or any other mood-altering substance or activity.

Alcoholics experience some guilt, but the primary thing they struggle with is shame. They are ashamed of their lives because they have lost control. Shame serves as a prison for addicted people. They feel locked up and alienated from the rest of society. They feel isolated and alone in their struggles. Shame, pain, and addiction all seem to work together in the battles an addicted person goes through. The apostle Paul describes this kind of personal struggle in Romans 7:15–20:

> I do not understand my own actions. For I do not do what I want, but I do the very thing I hate. Now if I do what I do not want, I agree that the law is good. But in fact it is no longer I that do it, but sin that dwells within me. For I know

that nothing good dwells within me, that is, in my flesh. I can will what is right, but I cannot do it. For I do not do the good I want, but the evil I do not want is what I do. Now if I do what I do not want, it is no longer I that do it, but sin that dwells within me.

One of the reasons Alcoholics Anonymous is so effective is that meeting together allows people to realize they are not alone in their struggles. When I attend open AA meetings with my friends in recovery, I always feel a strong level of connectedness with the others in attendance. Even though I do not share the disease of alcoholism with these people, I do share a common humanity with them. Whenever I am with people who readily admit that they are not okay and that they need God, I feel spiritually enriched. In twelve-step support groups, the eighth step states, "We made a list of all the persons we had harmed, and became willing to make amends to them." Step nine continues, "We made direct amends to such people wherever possible; except when to do so would injure them or others."[4]

These two steps demonstrate the process of repentance. Making amends to those we have wronged is another thing we need to pay more attention to in most churches. In the past, we have falsely believed that once God forgives our sins, we no longer have to be concerned about the impact our sins have had on others. The ninth step reveals sensitivity to those who have been victimized by our sins. It recognizes that sometimes as sinners we cross so many lines with others that it is no longer appropriate for us to try to reinitiate a relationship with them. Sometimes God calls us to apologize and then to respect the distance our sins have created. The focus of our repentance needs to be on the well-being of the other, not ourselves.

The mix of sin, shame, and pain in most of our lives can be complicated and challenging. God is concerned about and has great compassion for those of us who experience too much of this. First Peter 5:7 says, "Cast all your anxiety on [God], because he cares for you." Shame and pain are the primary issues that need to be addressed by grace. Therefore, we need to develop a broader, more dynamic understanding of grace that meets the multifaceted set of spiritual needs within all of our lives.

We need to preach more about grace, not guilt, and we need to embrace the compassion of Jesus in relationship to the hurting world in which we live. When we do this, the reputation of the church will change. People will expect to experience God's grace when they encounter our congregations. Grace will be extended to others, both inside and outside the church. The church will become known for love, compassion, and kindness. Healing will take place in the lives of those encountering this grace, and their lives will be strengthened and rebuilt. Grace will enable our churches to grow, primarily because it will allow us to grow as individuals. First Peter 4:10 encourages us to be good stewards of "the manifold grace of God."

Discipleship Step # 4

After doing a searching and fearless moral inventory, you may have already been inspired to make amends with some of the people you have hurt. The person with whom you shared your original inventory may be able to help you come up with a plan for making further amends, or for beginning this process, if you have not done so already. This process does not occur overnight. Take your time and begin reconciling relationships with those whom you feel most comfortable. Allowing God's grace to be a part of this process makes it less intimidating. God wants us to experience his grace more fully so that we can share it more completely.

In our quest to become honest to God disciples, it is also important to be aware of how much shame you are experiencing. A toxic level of shame in your life may lead to psychological disorders or compulsive and addictive behaviors that will threaten your life and distract you from discipleship. You must ask yourself if the shame in your life is at a nourishing or a toxic level. If your shame is at a toxic level, then you may need to seek healing on a deeper level. Acknowledging your shame with a pastor, spiritual director, or therapist, or in a twelve-step group will help you to begin dealing with it.

Long-term help by a spiritual director, a counselor, or a support group will help you to bring toxic levels of shame back to a more nourishing level with the help of God's grace. Nourishing levels of shame remind us that we need each other and God. Toxic levels make us defensive and lead us to become easily offended by others. They also keep us from being honest with God and others.

The extra help we receive from spiritual directors, counselors, or support groups can also allow us to focus more effectively on things like worship, fellowship, and ministry, which are essential discipleship activities. Balance is the key as we seek to rebuild our broken lives and as we seek to walk humbly with God as disciples of Jesus Christ. Many of us need the encouragement of helping professionals to take better care of ourselves. Problems arise, however, when individuals shift their entire focus onto themselves. A strong balance between serving others and taking care of ourselves is not only good for our psychological well-being, but also for our faithful discipleship. Jesus knew how to take care of himself by setting aside time for prayer and solitude. It is a good idea to follow his example as we seek to serve him.

Discussion Questions

1. What is pain? What is resilience?
2. In what way does some pain in childhood help individuals to develop resilience for adulthood?
3. What is the impact of too much pain in a child's life?
4. What happens when our shame and pain mix?
5. What is the difference between sin and abuse?
6. Why do victims of abuse sometimes become abusers themselves?
7. Why do Christians pay more attention to the sinful side of our lives than to the broken side?
8. Why do some people develop compulsive and addictive behaviors?
9. What can set us free from these compulsive and addictive behaviors?
10. How has our traditional definition of grace been too narrow and limiting with regard to our real-life experiences?
11. How can we begin to develop a broader and more multifaceted understanding of grace? What would happen if we did?

Eleven

Humility and Grace

I *recently had a conversation with a friend who admitted* that he had done many things wrong in his life but felt little guilt. I thought that maybe this was so because the things he had done wrong were not really all that bad. When I suggested this possibility, he rejected it. He indicated that he knew some of the things he had done were clearly wrong and shared that he was often surprised that he didn't feel more guilt for having done them. Though his church suggested that he should feel guilty, he did not. He had no problem admitting that he had "sinned and fallen short of the glory of God" and that he needed God's grace. He just didn't seek grace in order to rid himself of a guilty conscience. What he really felt was a lot of pain and shame from the years of abuse he experienced during his childhood, and he wanted to experience freedom from this shame and pain. His general feeling was that this shame and pain were holding him back and keeping him from being the person God wanted him to be.

Humility

Human beings have an innate desire for greatness that can be distorted by our shame. We all yearn for influence and prestige, and this desire can be productive, but it can also be destructive. It can lead us to pursue positive goals, but it can also lead us to become preoccupied with ourselves. As a result, we may sacrifice our positive goals for personal gain. Jesus teaches that humility is the path we must take if we want to be considered great in his kingdom. Jesus said, "Whoever wishes to be great among you must be your servant, and whoever wishes to be first among you must be your slave; just as the Son of Man came not to be served but to serve, and to give his life as a ransom for many" (Matt. 20:26–28).

Jesus had all authority, yet he used his authority humbly through service to lift up others. He chose not to "lord it over them," but rather to grab hold of their hearts through acts of humbleness. When Jesus washed his disciples' feet, he taught them that people in ministry should not see themselves as being above others. He was guarding their hearts and lives from the arrogance that he knew could ruin their future lives and ministries.

Several years ago an older woman in our community died. She was not connected with any local church, but I was asked to do her funeral. She had obviously lived a challenging life. She was a single mother at a time when single parenting was not as common as it is today. She also had to work long hours and a variety of physically challenging and unglamorous jobs to meet her family's financial needs.

While I was meeting with her family before the funeral, the children of this woman gave me a fascinating description of their mother. They beautifully described her as someone who respected others and who in turn received respect from them. They shared that she never saw anyone or anything as being beneath her. Many people perceive certain types of work as being beneath them and therefore think of those who do those jobs as being inferior. When Jesus washed the feet of his disciples, he demonstrated that if nothing is beneath him, then nothing and no one should be seen as beneath his disciples. John 13:5–8 describes his act of servanthood.

Then he poured water into a basin and began to wash the disciples' feet and to wipe them with the towel that was tied around him. He came to Simon Peter, who said to him, "Lord, are you going to wash my feet?" Jesus answered, "You do not know now what I am doing, but later you will understand." Peter said to him, "You will never wash my feet." Jesus answered, "Unless I wash you, you have no part with me."

Humiliation

Humility and humiliation often get confused, but they are actually very different. While teaching a confirmation class on humility, I once asked a group of middle school students what the difference was between humility and low self-esteem. One of the students said, "Nothing," indicating that they meant the same thing. But another student disagreed, saying that low self-esteem is related to humiliation, not humility. The second student got the point I was trying to make. Humiliation is something that leads you to feel bad about yourself. Humility addresses how you view and treat others. Humility helps to build self-confidence, whereas humiliation diminishes it.

In some cultures, people bow to one another as a symbol of humility and respect. Bowing shows high regard for other people as you greet them. I often teach the concept of humility with young people by using the image of bowing. I begin by asking two students to bow to each other. I then ask one volunteer to lie flat on the floor. Then I ask the person on the floor to bow to the other. This is obviously impossible. This exercise demonstrates the idea that you have to stand on your own two feet before you can bow. Likewise, you cannot allow people to walk all over you and still show humility. You must have inner strength in order to act humbly toward another person.

Humility is the missing link in much of modern Christianity. It is the key that can open the door to a more authentic Christianity. Placing the interests of others before our own goes against the grain of our culture, but it is this kind of counter-cultural thinking that should distinguish us as Christians. The apostle Paul writes in Philippians 2:3, "Do nothing from selfish ambition or conceit, but in humility regard others as better than yourselves." This verse does not speak of how we should think about ourselves. Rather, it speaks of how we should treat other people.

Imagine a society in which all people regarded others as better than themselves. We certainly would not face the entitlement issues we have today, because people would bear more responsibility for their own actions and attitudes. Furthermore, our self-esteem issues would dissipate because we would feel good about helping to build up other people. Others would, in turn, build us up. Galatians 6:2 says, "Bear one another's burdens, and in this way you will fulfill the law of Christ." Verse 5 then says, "All must carry their own loads." These two verses do not conflict with each other; they complement each other. Verse 5 simply insures that we will expect more from ourselves than we do from others. It is a safeguard against entitlement.

In twelve-step support groups, the tenth step states, "We continued to take personal inventory and when we were wrong, promptly admitted it." The eleventh step adds, "We sought through prayer and meditation to improve our conscious contact with God, as we understand God, praying only for the knowledge of God's will for us and the power to carry that out."[1] The general assumption in AA and other twelve-step programs is that we all have issues that will constantly need to be assessed and readdressed. If churches developed this same approach, we might be able to embrace grace more completely and share it with others more freely.

I have a friend who grew up going to a private Catholic school in the 1960s. One of the nuns at the school use to punish her and others by making them stand inside a garbage can in front of the class. This nun tried to shame her students into good behavior, but I am quite certain her method was not very effective. Humiliation never helps; it only hurts. Humiliation does not humble people. It harms them. When people are humiliated, they are made to feel worse about themselves. Humiliation often adds to the already dangerous levels of shame that exist in many people's lives.

Humiliation keeps people from being open and honest with others. It limits the amount of trust that can exist in relationships and work environments. Humiliation also gets in the way of the relationships people want to have with God. People who are humiliated on a regular basis often question their self-worth and have difficulty receiving God's love. Humiliation keeps people from facing their fears and dealing with their pain.

When we are made to feel bad about ourselves on a regular basis, we lose the confidence we need to face life's challenges. We become hesitant to ask questions or to introduce ideas in group settings. We become overly sensitive and easily offended by others. We have a difficult time trusting others, which in turn prevents them from trusting us. We all are capable of enduring some humiliation in our lives, but there is a point at which humiliation becomes destructive.

Arrogance

Humility helps us gain a proper perspective on our shame and to live free from unhealthy levels of it. Feeling good about accomplishments is a good thing, so long as it is not used as the foundation for conceit. Positive pride can help us build the strength and confidence we need for humility. It protects the positive, good, and beautiful parts of ourselves from being contaminated by shame. Positive pride builds confidence, while negative pride builds arrogance.

Arrogance is often perceived as strength, but in reality it is weakness. The lack of positive pride in one's life is often what leads a person to become arrogant. When people do not know what to do with their shame, they often try to pretend that they do not have any, and this leads into hubris. They know there is something wrong with them, but they act like nothing bothers them. They act perfect to compensate for the anxiety they feel with regard to their imperfections.

Thinking more highly of ourselves than we ought to think is dangerous business. Arrogance and conceit keep us from having positive relationships with family, friends, and coworkers, and from experiencing spiritual growth. To grow and learn, we must admit we have something to learn from others. This is why Jesus often warned us about arrogance and taught us that humility is the ultimate guard against it. In Luke 20:46–47, he warned his disciples, "Beware of the scribes who like to walk around in long robes, and love to be greeted with respect in the marketplaces, and to have the best seats in the synagogues and places of honor at banquets. They devour widow's houses and for the sake of appearances say long prayers. They will receive the greater condemnation."

Humility is meekness not weakness. There is a difference. It takes a great deal of strength to be humble. We are at our personal best when humility is a part of our lives, for humility calls us to be responsible and respectful. The call to regard others as better than ourselves is a call to be great in God's eyes. We are called to treat others the way we want to be treated. We are called to love them by putting their interests before our own. Humility moves us toward positive, nurturing relationships with each other and God. Humility is a God-honoring virtue. It immediately recognizes that we need God more than he needs us. It forces us to see grace as something God gives us out of love, not from the perspective that we have done anything to earn it.

Our culture has trained us to compare ourselves with those around us. We ask, who looks better, or worse? Who has the best car? Who has the best house, spouse, career, clothes, or hair? You name it—we compare it. But the things we compare are secondary to who we are and how we really feel about ourselves. We know this in our heads, but in our hearts we regularly pay more attention to things that really do not matter to us. Typically the more insecure we feel, the more we are drawn into comparison games.

In the parable of the Pharisee and the tax collector in Luke 18:10–14, we can see just how significant humility was in Jesus's eyes as they compare themselves with each other. Jesus said:

> Two men went up to the temple to pray, one a Pharisee and the other a tax collector. The Pharisee, standing by himself, was praying thus, "God, I thank you that I am not like other people: thieves, rogues, adulterers, or even like this tax collector. I fast twice a week; I give a tenth of all my income." But the tax collector, standing far off, would not even look up to heaven, but was beating his breast and saying, "God, be merciful to me, a sinner!" I tell you, this man went down to his home justified rather than the other; for all who exalt themselves will be humbled, but all who humble themselves will be exalted.

Humility is what allows us to receive grace and to see God as bigger than us. Humility is also related to seeing other people as equal in value to us. It is the bold recognition that God created *all of us* in his image, not just some of us. It is the recognition that Jesus died on the cross for *all of us*. Humility is not just the key to our salvation, but also the key to living an authentic Christian life. It is the means by which we move out of a bland form of moderation into a bold form of Christian discipleship.

Discipleship Step #5

In our quest to become honest to God disciples, we need to place a major emphasis on humility. Humility helps us to grow spiritually and to become better stewards of God's grace. We show humility to others by honoring them. Romans 12:10 says, "Love one another with mutual affection; outdo one another in showing honor." We Christians should become competitive with regard to how much honor we show to others. We honor people by expressing our appreciation for who they are and what they do.

A good place to start practicing humility is with those you have dishonored in the past. There may be people in your family, workplace, neighborhood, or community you have treated as beneath you. Think about ways you can show them honor. It is also important to honor those in today's society who typically do not receive it. We honor people by taking time out of our busy lives for them, by listening to them and learning from them. We honor people by showing them our respect and gratitude.

Be on guard against putting your acts of humility on display for others. At times acting anonymously can allow us to avoid turning our acts of humility into opportunities for arrogance or personal gain. Micah 6:8 says, "What does the LORD require of you but to do justice, and to love kindness, and to walk humbly with your God." Humility is a key to authentic discipleship. Showing honor to others on a regular basis is a great way to build up your humility without falling into the trap of self-righteousness. Think about how the reputation of the church might improve if people in the church were known for striving to outdo one another in showing honor.

Discussion Questions

1. What is humility?
2. What is the difference between humility and humiliation?
3. What is the difference between positive pride and negative pride? What is helpful about positive pride?
4. In what ways can a lack of inner strength keep you from being humble?
5. What is the difference between weakness and meekness?
6. From where do arrogance and conceit come? What is wrong with arrogance and conceit?
7. Why do people spend so much time and energy comparing themselves with one another?
8. What are some of the things that people like to compare?
9. How does comparing yourself with others get in the way of your relationships and spiritual development?
10. How does humility help you to receive grace and grow spiritually?
11. How can humility help us to become more gracious with others?
12. In what ways is humility a missing link within modern Christianity and a key to authentic Christian discipleship?

Twelve

Revolution and Acceptance

*A*fter I spoke at an adult retreat about grace and graciousness, a seventy-two-year-old woman came up to me and thanked me for what I shared. She then surprised me by saying, "Thank you for starting a revolution." Until that time I had not thought about grace and graciousness as being revolutionary. I only felt as if I was sharing the obvious about Jesus and the church. However, after considering her comment further, I began to accept that grace is, indeed, revolutionary. If we were to embrace it and let it flow fully out of our lives and churches, a spiritual revolution would inevitably be the result.

Grace should never be held back. We do not lose grace when we give it away. The more we give it away, the faster it replenishes itself. God provides us with an endless bank of grace, love, and power to share freely with others, both inside and outside of the church. This is the key for allowing a new kind of revolutionary discipleship to emerge.

God's Love

To help describe God's love to others, I use the image of an apple cut in half. The three most visible parts of the apple are the skin, the meat, and the core. The apple's skin represents our exterior selves—how we look on the outside. The meat of the apple represents the substantive part of our lives—the things we say and do. And the core part of the apple represents our core—the soul. Basic Christian theology readily recognizes that God cares most about the core part of who we are, yet in our society we still pay the most attention to our appearances. God is most concerned about the interior, while we are most concerned about the exterior. We care most about how we are being perceived, but God cares most about how things actually are. God cares most about the deeper things in life, whereas we tend to care most about superficial or shallow concerns.

God's focus is on the core part of who we are more than on the substance. Yet many of us want to please God with the substance of our lives. We want God to care about the things we say and do. The ego-driven part in us would prefer to get into heaven by our own goodness rather than God's. But we should rejoice that we have a God who loves the core more than the substance, or the skin. We have a God who loves the soul more than the ego, and who chooses to redeem us from the inside out. We need to realize that God loves us as we are so that we can begin to address the aspects of our lives that leave us feeling uneasy with the paths that we follow.

This is why God's grace and acceptance are so important. Realizing that God loves us as we are is an essential starting point in our discipleship. It is only after this realization that the power of God's grace can be released more fully into our lives. We need to realize that God loves us completely—from the top to the bottom, inside and out. There is no part of us that God does not love, even though there are aspects of our lives God does not like.

Acceptance

In the parable of the prodigal son, the younger son wasted his inheritance in "dissolute living." He found himself feeding pigs food that he wished he could have eaten himself. Luke 15:17–19 says, "When he came to himself he said, 'How many of my father's hired hands have bread enough to eat and to spare, but here I am dying of hunger! I will get up and go to my father, and I will say to him, "Father, I have sinned against heaven and before you; I am no longer worthy to be called your son; treat me like one of your hired hands."'"

What the young man experienced was shame, not guilt. He did not feel guilty, he felt hungry, and it was due to this hunger and fear that he was able to swallow his pride and return home.

> He set off and went to his father. But while he was still far off, his father saw him and was filled with compassion; he ran and put his arms around him and kissed him. Then the son said to him, "Father, I have sinned against heaven and before you; I am no longer worthy to be called your son." But the father said to his slaves, "Quickly, bring out a robe—the best one—put it on him; put a ring on his finger and sandals on his feet. And get the fatted calf and kill it, and let us eat and celebrate; for this son of mine was dead and is alive again; he was lost and is found!" And they began to celebrate.
>
> Luke 15:20–24

The father in this story does not even acknowledge his son's confession. After their embrace, the father interrupts his son and does not allow him to say the words, "Treat me like one of your hired hands." Actually, the father does not speak a single word to the son; he simply embraces him in joy, clothes him like royalty, and spontaneously throws a party. The parable of the prodigal son reveals foremost that we are welcome to come as we are to God's party regardless of our past. It reveals that shame is deeper than guilt and that acceptance is even deeper than forgiveness.

Imagine how the son must have felt. He came back hoping his father would accept him home as a hired hand but instead was welcomed home as his son—in spite of all that he had done wrong. It is worth pointing out that the younger son in the parable of the prodigal son represents the sinners and the tax collectors, while the older son represents the scribes and the Pharisees. The scribes and the Pharisees always complained about Jesus spending time with the tax collectors and sinners. Jesus spent time with these people because they were the ones he came to redeem. God wants sinners to return home. If we have always remained close to home like the Pharisees, then we must understand why those who have left must be welcomed home with bold acceptance, unconditional love, and joy-filled celebration.

The parable of the prodigal son is not so much about God's forgiveness as it is about his acceptance. Too many sermons have been preached on guilt in relationship to Genesis 3, and even more have been preached on forgiveness with regard to the parable of the prodigal son. Grace is much larger and more dynamic than either of these two interpretations. Grace not only forgives, but it also heals, liberates, strengthens, nourishes, welcomes, and offers acceptance and hope. Shame often leads us to believe we should be treated as servants, not children. God's grace reminds us that in spite of our sin, God still loves us as his own.

Serenity

We do not free ourselves from the bondage of shame; God does. Getting free from the bondage of shame is not a matter of self-acceptance, but rather a matter of accepting God's acceptance. It is not a matter of self-love, but of accepting the perfect love that God has for each one of us. Accepting God's acceptance is our way of receiving God's grace. It is our way of internalizing God's powerful presence within our lives. It enables us to experience his healing touch and allows us to enter fully into the process of redemption.

When I accepted Jesus into my life, I figured that if God could love me, then so could anyone else. And if others didn't love me, then that was their problem, not mine. I became less concerned with people's perceptions of me and more concerned with what God expected from me. I went from being someone who lacked confidence to someone who had confidence. I went from being someone who did not like himself to someone who understood that God loved and accepted him as he was. I went from being a follower in my peer group to being a leader. I felt like a new creation. My life felt much better than it ever had; I even felt sorry for some of the people I use to envy. I wanted them to know about God's grace too.

God's grace allows us to have serenity as followers of Jesus. Serenity comes when we accept God's acceptance of us, when shame is no longer the defining force in our lives. Serenity comes from the confidence we gain in Christ and from the clarity we develop about the purposes he has for us. Serenity comes when we stop comparing ourselves to others, when we stop worrying about what other people think and start being concerned about what God wants for us and from us. Serenity comes when we stop trying to hide ourselves and start truly being ourselves. Serenity comes from a life saturated by grace. As the twelfth step in twelve-step support groups states, "Having had a spiritual awakening as a result of these steps, we tried to carry this message to others, and to practice these principles in all our affairs."[1]

God's revolutionary work is about transformation, not condemnation. And God transforms us one person at a time. The apostle Paul urges us in 2 Corinthians 6:1 not to receive God's grace in vain. This is done when a person attempts to receive God's grace without taking full advantage of its power to help others and to respond to the needs of our world. Grace should be shared openly with others by being as gracious as we can be.

For this grace-based revolution to occur, we must take God's grace more seriously for ourselves, and our churches must share God's grace more assertively with others. The "I'm not okay, you're not okay" approach is effective because of its focus on people and its method of approaching them. It invites us to accept people as they are before we begin a relationship with them. It encourages us to offer them our acceptance as a means of introducing them to God's grace and love.

Moreover, for a grace-based revolution to occur, pastors and church leaders must begin to embrace grace for themselves and to allow grace to become the means by which we call people into the church and to support them once they arrive. Avoiding the extremes of the far left and the far right is not enough. We also need to pursue Christ and his ways passionately and compassionately. We need to find this pathway to God's grace and allow honest to God churches to emerge.

Discipleship Step #6

In our quest to become honest to God disciples and to develop honest to God churches, we need to become as gracious as we can possibly be to others. We need to start a grace-based revolution. Grace really does work in our lives and in the lives of others. I recently spoke with a lay leader from another church who, along with his pastor and other lay leaders from their church, attended a conference where I spoke about becoming grace-based churches. He shared that his church embraced this message and has never been the same since. Their church is growing and welcoming a broader range of people. Their pastor is offering the sacraments of grace more generously, which has been a key element in how welcoming and inclusive their church has become.

My hope for you and your church is that you will accept God's acceptance and become the honest to God disciples and churches God desires. God's grace is revolutionary, and we need to allow grace to have a revolutionary impact on our lives and our churches. If we recognize our own need for grace, then we should also be able to recognize the need other people have for it. This should inspire us to share grace assertively. If grace is the method through which God chose to minister to us, then grace ought to be the method we choose for ministry to each other. Our primary responsibility as disciples of Jesus Christ is to follow him and his ways. Grace and graciousness defined the life and ministry of Jesus. Therefore, grace and graciousness should also define our discipleship and provide our churches with a foundation for becoming the honest to God churches God wants them to be.

Discussion Questions

1. In what ways is the connection of grace and graciousness revolutionary?
2. Referring to the apple analogy, what part of your life are you most concerned about: the skin, the meat, or the core?
3. Why do you think God cares most about the core but many people care most about the skin?
4. How is shame deeper than guilt? How is acceptance deeper than forgiveness?
5. In what ways is God's grace about more than just forgiveness?
6. In the story of the prodigal son, why does the son return home?
7. Why did the father not allow the son to finish his speech? Which part does he keep him from saying?
8. What does the father offer the son upon his return?
9. What is the difference between self-acceptance and accepting God's acceptance?
10. How generously do you think pastors and church leaders should offer the sacraments of grace? Should the sacraments be used to leverage or influence the lives of individuals?
11. How can the "I'm not okay, you're not okay" approach help us to offer such things as grace, space, and acceptance more effectively?
12. What is the difference between moderate Christianity and the revolutionary Christian discipleship the author hopes will emerge from between the extremes?

Epilogue

*H*omosexuality *is one issue in the church today that clearly* tests our views on God's grace. Many people in our society do not understand homosexuality and don't care to put much time and effort into thinking about it. This issue, more than any other in my lifetime, has divided the church and created a situation in which individuals and congregations take sides and define themselves as either liberal or conservative. Sadly, denominations and local churches are falling apart because they are unable to find any middle ground on this issue. The extremes on the far right and the far left both seek to make the issue of homosexuality black and white, but it is far more complicated. Some people think God is using the controversy over homosexuality to purify their churches on the right or the left. I think the devil may be using it to divide and conquer the healthy churches in our midst.

While homosexuality is clearly challenging for our churches today, it would be a terrible mistake to allow this one topic to polarize our congregations and push us to the extremes on all other issues as well. My heart goes out to gay and lesbian people who want to be a part of a church but who do not feel safe or welcome in our congregations. My heart also goes out to churches and Christians who feel forced by their denominations to take a position with which they might not agree. Many members in my congregation hold views both to the right and left of mine. However, we all agree that our differences should not prevent us from participating in worship and ministry together. We also agree that this one issue should not keep us from focusing on all the other concerns confronting our lives, families, and world.

Recently I conducted a funeral service for a church member who I knew for years and cared about deeply. She was one of the most politically conservative people in our church. However, she also has a gay son who is in a committed, long-term relationship with another man. Her son came to church on a regular basis during the final year of her life. He used his mother's inability to drive as an opportunity to come to worship on a regular basis. It felt safer for him to come under this pretext rather than with his partner.

A few days before she died, she asked me point-blank if her son and his partner were welcome in our church. She did not want to know my position on homosexuality. She wanted to know if her child was welcome in the church she had belonged to and supported for so many years. She wanted to be able to tell her son that he and his partner were welcome before she died. I told her they were welcome, and I have had open and honest follow-up conversations with them about this. They have become a more active part of our congregation since then.

Gay and lesbian people are not problems to be solved. They are children of God created in God's image, just like all of us. These men and women are human beings worthy of God's love and grace. They are also worthy of our respect and acceptance and certainly do not deserve to be excluded or mistreated by members of the body of Christ. Churches are called to share the gospel with real people who have real issues. It is a mistake to allow one issue to harden our churches on either extreme. Doing so will limit the potential impact of the gospel on people's lives and keep us from ministering and worshiping effectively.

The "I'm not okay, you're not okay" approach works well for local churches where tension over such issues exist. This approach allows congregations to be open and welcoming to all people without forcing everyone in the community to come down in the same place on every issue. This approach allows for a creative balance between not condemning and not condoning similar to the one Jesus drew with the woman caught committing adultery. This woman was brought before Jesus by the scribes and the Pharisees to see if he would have her stoned to death. Jesus responded, "Let anyone among you who is without sin be the first to throw a stone at her." Those who brought her before him left without condemning her. John 8:9–11 says, "Jesus was left alone with the woman standing before him. Jesus straightened up and said to her, 'Woman, where are they? Has no one condemned you?' She said, 'No one, sir.' And Jesus said, 'Neither do I condemn you. Go your way, and from now on do not sin again.'"

Though Jesus did not condemn her, he did privately tell her to "go and sin no more." This text reveals that Jesus takes sin seriously but also that he cares more about the people who sin than the sin itself. The text also demonstrates his preference for private consultation over public condemnation when it comes to issues of human sexuality. The scribes and Pharisees treated this woman like an object, but Jesus treated her like a human being.

The gay and lesbian people I know who are still interested in the church desire acceptance as human beings, whether or not this includes full acceptance of their homosexual orientation. Homosexual people understand that a variety of opinions exist in our society and congregations surrounding the topic of homosexuality, but what they want is enough space in the church to allow God's grace to help them deal with all of their issues at their own pace and in their own ways. Sadly, many gay and lesbian people are no longer interested in the church because of the way they have been treated. So little compassion and understanding has been shown by the church that it is hard for them to see how God's grace can be obtained through it.

Homosexuality—or any other matter where controversy exists—should not get in the way of our call to be channels of God's grace for all people. Our call is to share God's grace, not to decide who gets it. We share this grace with broken people so that they can begin a journey toward wholeness, whatever that looks like. This is where the great divide in the church has formed over homosexuality. Some people believe that gay and lesbian people can be made whole with a homosexual orientation; others believe that they can only be made whole if they become heterosexual. My contention is that whether or not homosexual people see their sexual orientation as sinful, they can see themselves as sinners and begin the process of redemption referred to in this book. Consequently, we can treat all sinners the same way—as unique works in progress.

Many gay and lesbian people live with a great deal of pain. Some have endured abuse throughout their childhoods and into their adult lives. Some have been ostracized and alienated by their family and friends. Some have attempted suicide as they have struggled to deal with life and their sexual orientation. We Christians are called to offer hope to the broken people we encounter, no matter what is going on in their lives. I ask everyone in my church to be as compassionate and loving to the gay and lesbian people in our midst as they would be to anyone else, and I encourage all of us to remain focused on our own sins rather than on the sins of others. We need to take a searching and fearless moral inventory of our own lives. We do not need to do this for other people.

The "I'm not okay, you're not okay" approach simultaneously allows churches to welcome gay and lesbian people and allows for a variety of views on the homosexual issue to coexist. It allows churches to welcome all people without suspicion or hesitation, and it helps us to see that God calls us into loving solidarity with all humanity. Gay and lesbian people need God's grace as much as the rest of us. The church should never grow tired of finding ways to extend God's grace to those who need it most. We need to offer grace not judgment. James 2:13 says, "For judgment will be without mercy to anyone who has shown no mercy; mercy triumphs over judgment."

May the God of hope fill you with all joy and peace in believing, so that you may abound in hope by the power of the Holy Spirit.
—Romans 15:13

Notes

One
Grace and Graciousness

1. Michael Yaconelli, *Dangerous Wonder: The Adventures of Childlike Faith* (Colorado Springs: NavPress, 1998), 126.
2. Morton Kelsey, cited in Brennan Manning, *The Ragamuffin Gospel: Embracing the Unconditional Love of God* (Sisters, OR: Multnomah, 1990), 21.

Two
The Nice Church

1. Albert Nolan, *Jesus Before Christianity* (Maryknoll, NY: Orbis, 1992), 79.
2. Dallas Willard, *Renovation of the Heart: Putting on the Character of Christ* (Colorado Springs: NavPress, 2002), 238.

Three
Radical Not Fanatical

1. Tony Campolo, *Following Jesus without Embarrassing God* (Dallas: Word, 1997), 271.

Four
Passion and Compassion

1. Nolan, *Jesus Before Christianity*, 169.
2. Dietrich Bonhoffer, *The Cost of Discipleship* (New York: Macmillan, 1963), 97.

Five
Entitlement and Nullification

1. David Van Biema, "Does Heaven Exist?" *Time,* March 24, 1997, 71–78.
2. Kathleen A. Brehony, *After the Darkest Hour: How Suffering Begins the Journey to Wisdom* (New York: Holt, 2000), 118.

Six
Pain and Redemption

1. Brennan Manning, *The Ragamuffin Gospel: Embracing the Unconditional Love of God* (Sisters, OR: Multnomah, 1990), 27–28.

Seven
First Steps

1. Willard, *Renovation of the Heart*, 84–85.
2. John Bradshaw, *Healing the Shame That Binds You* (Deerfield Beach, FL: Health Communications, 1988), 125–26.

Eight
Sin and Shame

1. Bradshaw, *Healing the Shame*, vii.
2. Ibid., 3.
3. Lewis B. Smedes, *Shame and Grace: Healing the Shame We Don't Deserve* (New York: HarperCollins, 1993), To the Reader.

4. Ibid., 63.
5. Bradshaw, *Healing the Shame*, 127–28.

Nine
Secrets and Lies

1. Edwin H. Friedman, *Generation to Generation: Family Process in Church and Synagogue* (New York: Guilford Press, 1985), 52.
2. J. Keith Miller, *The Secret Life of the Soul* (Nashville: Broadman & Holman, 1997), 113.

Ten
Sin and Pain

1. Brehony, *After the Darkest Hour*, 14.
2. Ibid., 14.
3. Bradshaw, *Healing the Shame*, 15.
4. Ibid., 129.

Eleven
Humility and Grace

1. Bradshaw, *Healing the Shame*, 130–31.

Twelve
Revolution and Acceptance

1. Bradshaw, *Healing the Shame*, 131.